Joseph Moore

The Queen's Empire

Or, Ind and her Pearl

Joseph Moore

The Queen's Empire
Or, Ind and her Pearl

ISBN/EAN: 9783337173487

Printed in Europe, USA, Canada, Australia, Japan

Cover: Foto ©ninafisch / pixelio.de

More available books at **www.hansebooks.com**

THE QUEEN'S EMPIRE;

OR,

IND AND HER PEARL.

BY

JOSEPH MOORE, Jr., F.R.G.S.,

AUTHOR OF "THE EGYPTIAN OBELISKS," AND "OUTLYING EUROPE AND THE NEARER ORIENT;" MEMBER OF THE SOCIETY OF GEOGRAPHY OF PARIS, FELLOW OF THE AMERICAN GEOGRAPHICAL SOCIETY, MEMBER OF THE ROYAL ARCHÆOLOGICAL INSTITUTE OF GREAT BRITAIN AND IRELAND, MEMBER OF THE SCOTTISH GEOGRAPHICAL SOCIETY, ETC., ETC.

ILLUSTRATED WITH FIFTY PHOTOTYPES SELECTED BY
GEORGE HERBERT WATSON.

PHILADELPHIA:
J. B. LIPPINCOTT COMPANY.
LONDON: 15 RUSSELL STREET, COVENT GARDEN.
1886.

Copyright, 1885, by J. B. LIPPINCOTT COMPANY.

TO

GEORGE HERBERT WATSON,

IN REMEMBRANCE OF OUR MEETING IN COLORADO, OUR STRUGGLES WITH FRENCH
AT BLOIS AND GERMAN AT HANOVER, OUR HAPPY DAYS IN NEW
YORK AND PHILADELPHIA, AND OUR LONG
JOURNEY AROUND THE WORLD,

THIS VOLUME IS DEDICATED,

IN TOKEN OF THE

FRIENDSHIP OF A LIFE.

PHOTOTYPES BY

F. GUTEKUNST, PHILADELPHIA.

"Where'er I roam, whatever realms to see,
My heart, untravell'd, fondly turns to thee;
Still to my country turns, with ceaseless pain,
And drags at each remove a lengthening chain."

CONTENTS.

CHAPTER I.

AROUND THE WORLD.

An Auspicious Meeting—A Covenant—Plans of a Tour—Homage to Byron—A Tribute to Dean Stanley—The Rendezvous—Our Life at Blois—Dread News—Starting Eastward—A Glimpse of Vienna—Venice in Brief—On the Adriatic—Brindisi—A Chain-Gang—The Fortunes of Travel—Landing in Egypt—Motley Alexandria—Inundation of the Nile—Cairo from the Citadel—Royal Mummies—A Ride to Memphis—At the Pyramids—Along the Suez Canal—The Gate of Two Continents 15

CHAPTER II.

ON TROPICAL SEAS.

Bound for Bagdad—On Board the Steamer—Pilgrims for Mecca—Cholera Quarantine—Sinai in the Distance—Heat on the Red Sea—Routine on the Ship—Jewelled Nights—The Holy Land of the Prophet—Eve's Tomb—Arabian Ports—The Gate of Tears—Anchored at Aden—Strange People—The Diving Boys—Ostrich Feathers—A Dreary Stronghold—Massive Tanks—A Shadow on our Plans—Across the Arabian Sea—Death in the Cabin—Committed to the Deep—Ashore at Kurrachee—An Indian Bungalow—Sacred Alligators—Delay and Doubt—A Serious Disappointment—Travel in Asiatic Turkey—A Cargo from the Persian Gulf—End of the Voyage 38

CHAPTER III.

BOMBAY.

A New World—Novel Vehicles—Saturating Heat—Indian Hotel Life—Native Types—Features of the City—The Hospital for Animals—A Tropical Market—The Towers of Silence—Scavenger Birds—A Parsee Funeral—The Fire-Worshippers—Reverence for the Elements—The Hindu Burning-Place—A Funeral Pyre—Reducing a Body—Advantages of Cremation—The Snake-Charmer—A Clever Juggle—The Caves of Elephanta—A Rock Temple—Gods in Stone. 58

CHAPTER IV.

ACROSS INDIA BY RAIL.

Requisites for Travel—A Railway Station—Troublesome Coolies—Landscape Views—Female Porters—A Bullock Cart—Sketch of Surat—The Cotton Interest—Quaint Epitaphs—A Hindu Wedding—Nautch Girls and their Dance—Chewing the Betel—Native Salutes—Reverence for Europeans—Antipodal Customs—A One-Horse Shay—The Martial Rajpoots—A Modern Indian City—Royal Palace and Stables—Our First Rajah—A Street Picture—Buying Curios—The Makers of the Gods—An Elephant Ride—A Deserted City—Superstition's Edict 76

CHAPTER V.

CITIES OF THE MOGULS.

Imperial Delhi—The Mogul Dynasty—Splendors of the Fort—The Peacock Throne—Lalla Rookh and her Father—A Famous Bazaar—The Cathedral Mosque—A Jain Temple—Episode of the Mutiny—A Thrilling Struggle—Old Delhi

—A Wondrous Tower—Sumptuous Ruin—Crescent and Cross—A Peep at the Himalayas—Entering the Punjaub—The Koh-i-noor—An Indian Jehu—English Homes in Lahore—Longing for England—Noor Mahal and her Lover—Conquest of the Sikhs—The Shalimar Gardens—An Elephant Station—Beyond the Kyber Pass—The Golden Temple—Worship of the Sikhs—Cashmere Shawls—The Feast of Moharram—Agra—Mogul Magnificence—The Pearl Mosque—A Transitory Paradise—Akbar the Great and his Works—The Crowning Glory of India—An Ideal Creation—Dazzling Beauty of the Taj—Love's Altar and Tomb . 96

CHAPTER VI.

SCENES OF THE MUTINY.

Landscape of the Plateau—A Veteran's Tale—Cawnpore—Causes of the Mutiny—The English Unprepared—Besieged by Sepoys—Desperate Defence—Surrender and Massacre—The Satanic Nana—Fiendish Butchery—Tragedy of the Well—Avenging Heroes—Stern Retribution—Fate of Nana Sahib—Memorials of Sorrow—Slumbering Disloyalty—The Morale of India—Architecture of Lucknow—Outbreak in Oudh—The Historic Residency—Death of Sir Henry Lawrence—The Memorable Siege—Valorous Deeds—Relief and Joy—Coming of the Highlanders—Cutting their Way—Victory and Peace—A Knightly Soldier—Life's Work Well Done—In Memoriam 130

CHAPTER VII.

HOLY PLACES OF THE HINDUS.

The City of God—A General Centre—Festival of the Mela—Habits of the Fakirs—A Sceptical Lion—The Tree of Knowledge—American Missionaries—Three Sacred Places

—Entering the Holy City—Sanctity of Benares—India in Profile—Street Scenes—The Great Temple—Consecrated Bulls—Linga Stones—The Brahmins—Hindu Deities—Pagan Rites—Profitable Idols—The Well of Fate—An Obscene Shrine—The Monkey Temple—Sacrifice of a Goat—The Stay of Hinduism—Its Four Castes—Brahmin Power—A Devout Maharajah—Visiting in State—A Prince's Hospitality—The Buddhist Holy Land—Bathing in the Ganges—A Striking Picture—The Burning Ghaut—Outward Piety—A False Religion—Venality of the Priests—An Essay by Brahmins—They Defend their Faith—The Opposite View—A Voice from the Zenana Mission—Blind Faith 152

CHAPTER VIII.

THE INDIAN CAPITAL.

Across Bengal—Tigers and Thugs—Puny Bengalees—Poverty in a Rich Country—Expensive Government—The City of Palaces—A Calcutta Hotel—Our First Earthquake—The Aristocratic Quarter—An Evening Drive—The Black Hole—Palms and Banyans—The Temple of Kali—A Bought Sacrifice—Brahmin Degradation—The Native Quarter—A Maharajah's Palace—Educating the Natives—The Most Promising Path—Zenana Missions—A Woman's Work—Converts in Church—The Viceroy's Court—Social Gayeties 189

CHAPTER IX.

IN THE HIMALAYAS.

Seeing the Hills—Journeying Northward—Over the Ganges—A Miniature Railway—Home of the Tiger—Ascending the Mountains—A Prospect of Grandeur—Novelty of Cold—The Loop—Frightened Pigs—New Faces—Ferns and

Oaks—Equal to any Feat—A Lofty Village—Prayer Flags—Dangerous Curves—Picturesque Darjeeling—Our Damsel Porters — Persistent Clouds—Market Day— Himalayan Tribes—Portrait of a Bhotea—Conjugal Relations—The Lamas—A Praying Machine—The Jewel is in the Lotus—Pagan Ceremonies—Mongolian Types—The Warlike Ghorkas—An Afternoon's Tramp—A Tea Plantation—Pruning the Vines—Preparing the Leaves—Green and Black Tea—Growth of the Plant—A Cloudless Morning—The Roof of the World—An Early Ride—A Hiding Cloud—On Mount Senchal—A Sublime Panorama—The Pinnacle of the Earth—Holiest of Communions 202

CHAPTER X.

THE MADRAS PRESIDENCY.

Adieu to the Abode of Snow—Embarking at Calcutta—In the Hoogly—A Gorgeous Pilot—Our Rash Passenger—The Car of Juggernaut—Along the Coast—A Race against the Sun—An Appeal for Welcome—The Madras Surf—An Abortive Breakwater—A Boat without Nails—Riding the Breakers—Outline of Madras—A Familiar Name—Lack of Attractions—An Oppressive Climate—Great Rock Temples—Sculptured Pagodas—The Dravidian Family . . . 222

CHAPTER XI.

CEYLON, THE PEARL.

A Catamaran—An Amphibious Creature—Sighting the Island—A Double Canoe—View in the Harbor—Intense Heat—The Effeminate Singalese—Shops of the Moormen—Point de Galle — Luxuriant Beauty—Cinnamon—Her Majesty's Mail Stage—The Southern Cross—A Dashing Pace—Rosy Dawn—A Wealth of Nature—Twenty Million Palms—Betel-Chewing Etiquette—In and Around

Colombo—Tortoise-shell and Gems—Coffee-Curing—Pearl-Fishing—Diving for the Mollusks—Precarious Profits—Railway to the Interior—Prolific Vegetation—A Myth of Adam—The Coffee Belt—Dr. Holmes's Breadfruit—Uses of the Cocoanut Palm—The Highland Capital—A Sanitarium—Ruins of Ancient Cities—The World's Oldest Tree—An Exalted Shrine—The Buddhist Scriptures—A Golden Idol—Man's Future State—The Inner Sanctuary—A Momentous Relic—History of the Tooth—Five Hundred Million Worshippers.................. 231

CHAPTER XII.

RARE EXPERIENCES.

Kandy in Gala Dress—The Young Princes of Wales—Their Arrival and Reception—The Feast of the Perahara—Elaborate Preparations—Orgie of the Coffee-Planters—The Great Procession—A Weird Spectacle—Antics of the Devil Dancers—Native Chiefs—Elephants and Oriental Trappings—An Elephant Hunt for the Princes—Arrangements to Participate—Start from Colombo—Night on the Road—A Wayside Rest-house—An Outpost of the Camp—Afoot in the Jungle—Our Palm Huts—Evanescent Kraaltown—Locality of the Hunt—Construction of the Corral—Stratagem against Strength—A Cordon of Beaters—Watching the Game—An Unwonted Grouping—Night in the Camp—A Cobra Alarm—Docile Monsters—Uses of the Elephant—In Full Cry—At Bay in the Jungle—Man against Brute—A Native Crushed—The Drive-In—Infuriated Captives—A Premature Movement—Failure, Delay, and Success—Twelve in the Toils—Trained Elephants to the Front—Charge and Repulse—A Cow Noosed—Her Struggles and Death—Dragging and Tying a Victim—Two Orphan Calves—A Cowardly Tusker—Disposing of the Prizes—Eastward to the Golden West............. 257

LIST OF ILLUSTRATIONS.

	PAGE
Festival of the Perahara . . . . *Frontispiece.*	
Map of India and Ceylon	15
Blois, from the Chateau	18
The Graben, Vienna	22
In the Suez Canal	36
The English Stronghold of Aden	46
A Street in Bombay	58
The New Quarter of Bombay	62
A Parsee Family	66
A Hindu Burning-Place	70
Snake-Charmers	72
The Caves of Elephanta	74
An Indian Equipage	80
A Sweetmeat-Shop of Surat	82
Nautch Girls	86
Wind Palace and Bazaar, Jeypore	90
The Deserted City of Ambher	94
Hall of Private Audience, Delhi	98
The Great Bazaar of Delhi	100
The Jumna Mosque, Delhi	102
The Kootub Minar, Old Delhi	104
Ruins of Old Delhi	106
Lahore, Capital of the Punjaub	112
The Golden Temple, Umritsur	116
Exterior of the Agra Fort	120
Akbar's Palace, Agra	122
The Taj Mahal, from the Garden	124
The Taj Mahal, from the Terrace	128
Scene of the Massacre, Cawnpore	136

LIST OF ILLUSTRATIONS.

	PAGE
Entrance to the Bazaar, Lucknow	144
Gate of the Kaiser Bagh, Lucknow	148
Remains of the Presidency, Lucknow	150
Favorites of the Zenana	158
Quadrangle of the Golden Temple, Benares	162
The Monkey Temple, Benares	168
Tower at Sarnath, Buddhist Holy Land	172
The Burning Ghaut, on the Ganges, Benares	178
Types of Indian Servants	190
The Principal Street of Calcutta	194
Native Boats at Kalighat, Calcutta	198
A Hill Sanitarium	204
Palace and Temples of a Himalayan Village	210
A Tea Plantation, Darjeeling	216
Kanchinjanga, the World's Second Mountain	220
Business Quarter of Madras, with the Mole	226
Façade of a Dravidian Temple, Trichinopoly	230
Temple of the Sacred Tooth, Kandy	250
Group of Singalese Chiefs, Kandy	258
Entrance to the Kraal	266
Plan of the Kraal	268
Elephants Handling Timber	272
Noosing Wild Elephants	278

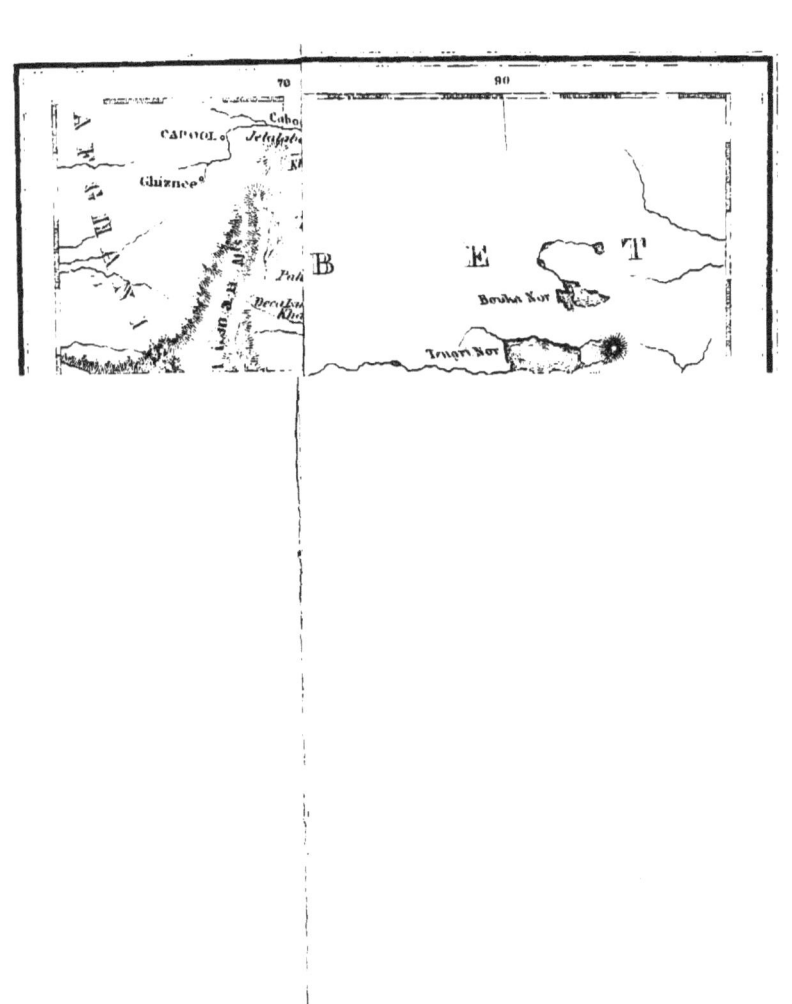

THE QUEEN'S EMPIRE;

OR,

IND AND HER PEARL.

CHAPTER I.

AROUND THE WORLD.

> The world thou hast not seen, much less her glory,
> Empires, and monarchs, and their radiant courts,
> Best school of best experience, quickest insight,
> In all things that to greatest actions lead.
> MILTON.

ONE afternoon in the summer of 1879, while it was raining a torrent, I boarded a belated train at Colorado Springs, bound for Denver. A wash-out had caused a delay of nearly two hours, and the chance of further danger made it necessary to run much slower than the usual speed. Night came, but no supper. As I had eaten nothing since a hasty dinner, shortly after noon, I inquired of the conductor how far it was to the next restaurant station. He curtly replied that it would be Denver, about midnight. Thereupon I complained roundly, and a gentleman occupying a neighboring seat joined in the wail. After the conductor had left, a conversation with my fellow-passenger followed. The next afternoon found us dining together at Denver, and on the following day we parted at Cheyenne,— pledged to meet again for a tour of the world.

Almost two years elapsed without sight or word of each other, and during that interval both were abroad. In the spring of 1881 our plans were matured in New York. Paris, late in the following July, was the rendezvous.

My previous wanderings had extended from the Suez Canal to the Golden Gate. Embraced in the detail were a circuit of the countries bordering on the Mediterranean and every state of Europe. Now I was anxious to see the storied lands and ancient civilizations so richly clustered in Asia proper.

Our proposed course after leaving Europe was conditionally outlined. First a brief review of Lower Egypt. Then a long voyage from Suez to Bagdad, ascending the Persian Gulf and the rivers Tigris and Euphrates, to trace the ruins of Nineveh and Babylon; and possibly, afterward, those of

Persepolis. Thence to Bombay, to traverse the mighty empire which lies south of the Himalayas. After we should reach Calcutta, the itinerary would be adapted to the requirements of time. As circumstances permitted, to include or omit Ceylon, Burmah, Java, Siam, Cochin China, and Cambodia. Upon starting northward from Singapore, the accepted half-way station, we were to devote a sufficient period to China and Japan before embarking for California.

If auspicious news from home should greet us upon landing at San Francisco, we would undertake the Yellowstone Park, the uncompleted Northern Pacific Railroad, and the Great Lakes, as a new track across the continent. Making this tour solely in the interest of education and experience, and by no means for pleasure, we anticipated many a weary, homesick day. Still we did not despair of those bright incidents, genial companionships, and absorbing scenes which always reward a traveller, and encourage him in his varied task. Some of these kaleidoscopic views, as they were realized, we shall here attempt to portray by picture and by pen.

Mindful of the engagement already stated, early in July, 1881, I sailed from New York. From Liverpool I went directly to Nottingham, to make the oft-deferred pilgrimage to Newstead Abbey and the little church at Hucknall, to do homage to the magnetic genius of the greatest, worst-abused poet of this century. A meteoric life with all the frailties of youth and passion, yet withal far nobler, far more exalted in character and generous in heart than those who have sought to defame his dazzling memory.

Thence my path was to London, where I arrived just in time to look down the open grave of Arthur Penrhyn Stanley, in his own beloved historic Abbey,—England's model churchman and free Christian, who believed in that broad Christianity which springs from the heart and not from mundane forms. Next I made a flying trip to the Isle of Wight, where, drawn by a tough gray cob in a dog-cart, I enjoyed flitting visions of rocky headlands, greenswards, picturesque towns, and breaking surf.

Without further digression I crossed to Paris. There, true to appointment, was my companion for the long tour; since then the chosen partner of many a journey, enterprise, and happy day. After a week in the urban Elysium, we went together to Blois, and rented a delightful châtelet on the bank of the Loire, just without the town. Within sight

BLOIS, FROM THE CHATEAU.

from our windows was the stately chateau where Francis I. lived, the Duc de Guise was murdered, and Catherine de Médicis breathed out her wicked life. In this quiet retreat we lived two profitable months studying French and the East, fishing and sailing, and driving to the princely chateaux in the vicinity,—Chambord and Beauregard, Chaumont, Amboise, and Chenonceaux.

Like every American—ay, like all mankind—we daily awaited with anxiety, now with fear, then with hope, the bulletins from the world's patient at Washington and Long Branch. While we were preparing to leave Blois, the dreaded message came, and we knew that the illustrious sufferer was at rest, that our beloved President was dead. We had received a crushing blow; we were plunged into a profound sorrow; our very homes seemed to be invaded by calamity and death, and the impulse was to return at once to stand in the horrible breach,— for what? To grieve with a stricken people, to hang out the emblems of mourning, and wonder what punishment the assassin could undergo sufficient to expiate so execrable a crime. Vain help to replace a murdered Garfield! But surely if a sparrow cannot fall to the ground without Divine intent, what infinite beneficence may be wrought by the martyrdom of the purest among the leaders of men.

We were glad enough when the October evening came upon which our tour was to commence, as we had already been delayed a day because the sleeping-car to Vienna was full, and there was no second one in a great terminus like Paris to supply the deficiency. As we crossed the Place de l'Opéra, bound for the Gare de Strasbourg, and soon after rolled away from the brilliant city, we began to realize the magnitude of the task ahead.

What might occur in our homes and country while we were beyond the reach of news! Would we both return in health and safety? What sacrifices were we making by our absence, and how great would be the benefits, valuable in after-life, to be derived from another year of exile, with its monotonous voyages, dusty journeys by rail, and the climatic risks of the torrid Orient? But away all doubts! The train is speeding eastward, and in that direction, for once, the star of empire, the empire of knowledge and experience, calls us with irresistible force.

When daylight came, the spire of the Strasburg Cathedral towered majestically over the plain, as we approached the disputed, armed Rhine, that beauteous river which is at once the source of plenty and want, joy and sorrow, wine and war, life and death. Away we sped through Carlsruhe and Stuttgart and Munich, recalling the days when, toiling by rail and by river, I traversed the Fatherland from quaint Lübeck to where the lion guards the lake at Lindau, and from Königsberg, on the northeast, to Heidelberg on the southwest. Towards midnight we were undergoing the usual visitation of luggage on the Austrian frontier, and early the next morning we alighted at Vienna.

As we had a week to spare before the departure of our steamer from Venice, or ten days if we joined her at Brindisi, we decided to go to Vienna, because my companion had not yet seen that city. Altogether, the visit was a disappointment, probably owing to the damp, cold weather and the trying comparison with Paris, which we had just left,—the one, *only* Paris of this globe. To see Vienna aright, it must be when the world is out of doors, drinking the clear, delicious beer and reading the little journals before the *cafés*, on the Ringstrasse, in the Graben, the Prater, the Volksgarten, and the thousand other spots where the pleasure-seeking Viennese love to congregate and enjoy life, as they understand it, to its fullest measure. It was thus I saw it upon coming down from Russia and Poland, after a wearisome period of draggy travel; and then, with its splendid new buildings, cheerful hotels, sunny parks, and genial atmosphere, it seemed, indeed, almost the peer of peerless Paris.

We took the new and more direct route to Venice, by Leoben, although it is probably less interesting than the other. Unfortunately, a heavy fog obscured the scenic glories of the Semmering Pass, but we fared better in the Lower Tyrol. Again, as the train approached the Italian border we ran into a brisk snow-storm, which had whitened the villages, covered the road to the depth of an inch or more, and draped the foliage with a boreal fringe. This was our first glimpse of winter and the last, except upon mountain-tops. Our effects easily passed inspection at the Italian frontier, and quite as easily was the alleged dinner disposed of which they offered us at the same station, as there was so little to eat. We reached Venice towards midnight, tired and satiated with thick sandwiches and coffee, yet hungry for something rather more inviting.

Silently the two gondoliers plied their oars, dipping into the moonlight upon the Grand Canal,

THE GRABEN, VIENNA.

while we, within the sombre hood, mused upon the mutations of life, which had brought us again so unexpectedly to the city of romance, intrigue, and song,—us who, a few years back, had so little prospect of wandering over the world, seeking out travellers' shrines in distant lands. But it is always the unexpected that happens, says Mme. de Sévigné, and the same charming authority declares that "life is too short to halt too long in one frame of mind." And our revery speedily gave place to reality as we were ushered into rooms in the attic of the leading hotel. Venice was full of tourists.

The following morning we went afoot to St. Mark's Square, a short walk, and renewed our acquaintance with its many attractions: its alluring shops, the clock-tower, the myriad of tame pigeons, St. Mark's Tower, the Doge's Palace, "the winged Lion's marble piles;" and, lastly, but the greatest of all, the wondrous church, with its confusing, yet harmonious, unexampled, and striking architecture. Within, the usual motley comers yet linger beneath its mosaic domes,—humble devotees counting their beads and sight-seers with the inevitable red books, shaven friars and Umberto's officers with clanging sabres, artists absorbed in their rich studies and the ubiquitous, pestering guides. Later in the day we took a gondola and glided slowly beneath the Bridge of Sighs and the Rialto, along the Grand Canal to its mouth, and before the city front. In the evening we again sauntered around the square, and returned content to board our ship, which lay in the harbor, the next morning.

We had originally intended to sail from Brindisi for Alexandria, but the prospect of twenty-four hours continuous travel by rail along the coast, without sleeping-cars, induced us to embrace the privilege offered by our tickets to embark from Venice. Upon boarding the steamer, the "Bangalore," of the Peninsular and Oriental line, our spirits were depressed by the discovery that, in addition to a ship no longer modern, we were located in a state-room with four berths. The Parisian agency, at which we had hurriedly engaged our passage, cunningly had no plan of the cabins to show. We knew the ship would be entirely full, as the autumnal hegira to Egypt and India had already commenced, and we dreaded the possibility of entering warm latitudes, so early in the season, with perhaps sea-sick Orientals, however exalted their social rank. We were somewhat relieved upon being told that the bulk of the passengers would join the ship at Brindisi, with our state-room companions among the number; and so, in comparative comfort, we saw St. Mark's Tower gradually sink into the horizon as the "Bangalore" carefully threaded her way through the lagoon and out the Lido.

Our first day upon the Adriatic brought with it rather doleful anticipations of the indefinite amount of ship-life before us, as the "Bangalore," only partly laden, rolled and pitched without respite. To add to our discomfort the leaden clouds dashed us again and again with heavy showers. Towards nine in the evening we sighted the Ancona light, and an hour later a myriad of twinkling glimmers resolved themselves into the town,—a medley of Italian houses climbing the hills from the shore,—before which, though scarcely in any harbor, the ship anchored until morning. The weather continued unfavorable throughout the second day and night, but cleared and grew perceptibly warmer the next morning, when we ran into the port of Brindisi.

Glad to escape a few hours from the uninviting ship and her wretched cuisine, with its coffee of lye and tea of tannin, we took a boat and were rowed ashore to the hotel, where we refreshed ourselves with a bath and an edible breakfast. There is little of interest at Brindisi. Most of the town is new and straggling, and the irrepressible cicerones about the hotel, as well as the drivers of a few dilapidated hacks and scrawny horses, annoy passengers throughout their brief stay. The constant cry about a traveller's ears is, "I am speak beautiful English; you want going at the post," or the "P. and O. bureaus," or, perhaps, "You wish go seen Appian Way?" As the ship was to remain until early the next morning, we took a front room at the hotel, overlooking the harbor, and devoted several hours to our correspondence.

Just as the sun was setting, with all the wondrous glow of an Italian sky, a long boat, filled with men and propelled by many an oar, slowly approached the quay and landed her cargo of wretched human freight, guarded by a squad with carbines slung ready for instant use. It was the first chain-gang I had ever seen. With a sullen demeanor, and not without some wrangling, the convicts formed a double file. Each was shackled by the ankle and wrist to a long chain, with which they marched away in the midst of the guards, clanking and proclaiming their crime alike to countrymen and strangers. There were young men, scornful, defiant, reckless; men in their prime, with neither past nor future to contemplate with joy; and old men, bleached with years or hardship, whose evening of life had come without that lamp of love, rest, and home which is the cheering light of declining years.

We went aboard again late in the evening and found our worst fears realized. The two berths in our state-room were occupied, and one by a tawny Egyptian, Mohammed by name, the counterpart of our Smith or Jones, an astrologer by profession and an unwelcome nuisance in general. Now, what was to be done? The ship was crowded; a hundred and one saloon passengers, although fifty-four was the ancient craft's complement. The excess, at full rates, were disposed of in second-class berths and fed in a dungeon politely designated as the lower cabin. The night was hot, but old Alkali Bey, as we entitled him, who had the berth beside the two ports, was dreadfully afraid of a chance breath of heated Italian air,—he called it a draft,— and so the ports had to remain closed.

We postponed retiring until it became a necessity, and by that time the odor of the venerable Arab and his musk, aided by the presence of a snoring Sicilian, had enriched the atmosphere of the state-room in a direction not conducive to refreshing sleep. One night of it was enough, and after that we slept on deck, undisturbed by either heat or cold, in the balmy air of the southern latitudes.

Stormy weather came upon us soon after we cleared from Brindisi, and so great was the pitching that the voyage was prolonged nearly a day, through the slip of the propeller. We passed close to the mainland of Greece and near two or three of its islands; but the gilding of their eternal summer, as Byron expresses it, was shrouded by the heavy skies which mark the change of seasons. Our passengers, with some few exceptions, were uninteresting, especially as many were sea-sick. However, we found pleasant companionship with Mr. W. M. Flinders Petrie, the English Egyptologist and author, who has spent two winters in making an accurate survey of the Ghizeh pyramids, aided more or less by Dr. Birch, of the British Museum, and the Royal Society of London. We also had several consuls and other officials returning to their posts after the summer vacation, who entertained each other in discussing Arabi's *coup d'état*, with the probable changes it would cause.

The old "Bangalore" tumbled slowly along, until on the afternoon of the fourth day out from Brindisi we were gladdened by a sight of the low coast of

Africa, followed by the modern Pharos of Alexandria and Pompey's Pillar. The Arab pilot cautiously guided us through the long mole into the harbor, and finally brought the ship to rest beside the new stone quay. Truly a great improvement upon the former method of landing in boats, amid the bedlam raised by the natives struggling for patronage. After a little annoyance from the howling Arabs, we cleared our luggage and readily evaded the demand for our passports, as we had no idea of being detained to search for them in some Oriental circumlocution office.

On the way to the hotel the bony horses, attenuated by a lack of fodder and the recent burning heat of Afric's summer, became stalled in attempting to cross the projecting track of the railway. In about five seconds we were out of that omnibus shouting to a slowly-approaching engine to halt. A strong pull, all together, extricated us from the snarl, and the noisy trap hurried away to the hotel on the Place Mehemet Ali, greeted by scores of children along the untidy streets. Evidently we were among the first of the winter travellers, after the long summer dearth.

The sensation upon landing in Egypt a second time, although less novel, was even more profound than the first. I had learned by the previous visit, and by subsequent study, the supreme interest centred in this land of Mizraim, of the Pharaohs, and of the Ptolemies, the very "first in the race that led to Glory's goal." There is, however, little inspiration in Alexandria,—foul, crowded streets, mongrel population, lack of historical relics, and absence of amusements. True it is a busy place, with all shades of Levantines hurrying to and fro, with its moneyed men shouting on the bourse and in the maritime exchange. But much of this is European, and not what we long to see in Egypt.

We drove to the spot where for centuries the two obelisks were, which now lend their ancient dignity to the metropolises of Great Britain and America. Then our way took us along the favorite road by the Mahmodieh Canal, and lastly to Pompey's Pillar, upon the hill, by the Mohammedan cemetery. So repulsive are the surroundings of this celebrated monolith, while the monument itself is in a sadly dilapidated condition, that its effect upon travellers is usually one of disappointment, especially if the observer has had the giant shaft heralded to him from childhood as one of the great sights of the world, as is frequently the case.

The next morning we were ready to take the

early train for Cairo, and as the sky was overcast and saved us from the glaring sun, the day proved auspicious for the journey. As the annual inundation was at about its highest level, nearly everywhere the fertile fields of the Delta were partly or wholly submerged. In some places the fellaheen were sowing the winter crop, where the water had been made very shallow through the intervention of the dykes, high or low, which traverse the country in squares.

Although the Nile directly overflows the ground upon its borders, such is not the case with that more distant. Egypt is a net-work of canals, basins, and embankments, by means of which the distribution of the "gift of the Nile" is governed by engineers appointed for the purpose. The water remaining in the embryo lakes after the soil in their vicinity has received its requisite deposit of the dark Abyssinian mud, or when the inundation has subsided, is either allowed to run into the river or is retained for later use.

Often we saw the mud villages perched upon hillocks, completely isolated by the flood, and the tawny inhabitants wading to them with their scanty clothing upon their heads. The sky cleared as we went southward, and when we arrived at Cairo, about the middle of the afternoon, unacclimated as we were, the rays of the sun, in the pure, dry atmosphere, penetrated like the heat of a fire.

Cairo! The beautiful, the gay, the curious! Few travellers remain indifferent to its charms, and fewer leave it without regret. The three brief years which had elapsed since I first beheld an Egyptian sunset from the citadel, looking over the minareted city of the Caliphs and Memlooks to the stately pyramids of the primeval monarchy, the oldest of the old, had not in the slightest effaced from my memory the splendor of the vision. Now as we approached the eyrie beside the imposing mosque of Mohammed Ali, I experienced the ardor of one who knows well the magnificence of the panorama which awaits him. The union of the ancient, the mediæval, and the modern; the bounteous Nile and its half-mystic, half-historic monuments; the prolific valley, framed in parched, stony hills and burning deserts; the crowded city, throbbing with life and pointed with the spires of faith; a living picture of the Arabian Nights; a vivid realization of the gorgeous Orient!

Alone we threaded the great bazaars, refusing the pretended aid of the commission-loving dragomans, and yielded to the temptations offered by strange wares and chance antiquities. Next we spent a morning in the Boulak Museum, of which Brugsch Bey is the able curator, and there saw the most important of the mummies recently discovered beneath the Temple of Dayr-el-Bahree, at Thebes. Among them are those of Aames I., the founder of the New Empire and first king of the eighteenth dynasty; Thothmes III., the great Sethi I. and his famous son, Rameses II., the Pharaoh of the Jewish captivity. Besides, there are the rich cases enclosing the bodies, garnished with hieroglyphics, gilding, and colors, as bright almost as when they were executed fifteen hundred years before Christ.

Making an early start one morning and taking donkeys with us, we went by train to Bedreshayn. Riding along the embankments above the inundated fields, we crossed the site of dead Memphis and explored the sculptured tombs, the marvellous Serapeum, or sepulchre of the sacred bulls, and the pyramids of Sakkara, the earliest structures of any kind now in existence.

The native children, innocent of clothing, followed us by the score, clamoring for baksheesh and urging us to drink from their water-jars, and caravans of Bedouins greeted us with the triple salutation of the Muslim as they passed towards the river, driving their strings of camels. High up in the tall date-palms the lithe Arabs, girded to the trees by ropes, were gathering in baskets the great clusters of ripe fruit. These they spread upon the ground in little wicket enclosures to dry.

After lunching in the house of the late Mariette Bey, his residence during the work of excavating at Sakkara, we again mounted the donkeys and rode along the edge of the desert to Ghizeh. Here we halted beneath the battered face of the kingly Sphinx, that faithful guardian of the necropolis, which has almost outlasted time itself. After seeing the granite temple, the rock tombs, and the remains of the causeway upon which the forgotten builders of the pyramids dragged up the great stones from the river, we rode around to the entrance of Cheops.

Of course, the ascent had to be made, assisted by the usual troublesome Bedouins. Upon descending we met Mr. Petrie, the archæologist, by appointment, and with him penetrated the interior to both the king's and the queen's chambers. Within, our special attention was given to the unique and surprising features of the masonry, with which Mr.

INCIDENT AT THE PYRAMIDS. 35

Petrie has become very familiar by prolonged observation and study.*

Upon reaching the middle of the north face of the Great Pyramid, as just related, we saw with indignation the name of an old American nostrum painted in huge black letters, then scarcely dry, on the stone above the entrance. In fact, the desecrator had only left the ground within two or three hours, after stating his purpose similarly to disfigure the ruins up the Nile. As I was aware that the patent compound thus disgracefully advertised had originated in my own city, and is probably yet prepared there,—although its former owner, now a pitiful spectacle, bought it notoriety while living in the metropolis,—we begged Mr. Petrie to have the offensive daubing removed, at our expense.

Our time in Egypt was necessarily brief, as we were booked for the Persian Gulf by the steamship "Canara," of the British India Steam Navigation Company, which was almost daily expected in the Suez Canal from London. It was therefore no cause for surprise when, on the third day of our

---

* Since returning home, I have had the pleasure of receiving from Mr. Petrie a copy of his exhaustive and learned work, "The Pyramids and Temples of Ghizeh." He settles forever the heretofore vexed question of the measurements of these monuments.

stay in Cairo, we received telegrams advising us to proceed to Suez, as the ship was already at Port Saïd. Our train left Cairo towards noon, and stopped at the Zagazig junction, amid a confusion of trains and a multitude of noisy tongues, for a late lunch or dinner, and about sundown we ran into Ismaïlia, midway on the canal.

Thence to Suez, nearly three hours' ride, the railway follows the line of the Fresh-Water Canal, by which Suez is supplied. In some places it passes near De Lesseps's highway, but over territory struggling between the arid desert and a narrow belt of partial fertility imbibed from scanty touches of the Nile in the Fresh-Water Canal. No conveyance of any description met the train at Suez, so we were compelled to tramp through the dark, unpaved, dusty streets to the hotel on the coast, followed by a squad of chattering coolies bearing the luggage.

Suez is a miserable, broiling town with a foul bazaar and rapacious venders of coral and mother-of-pearl. The terminal works of the Suez Canal, the artificial harbor, and the associations of the Exodus, comprise its capital for the entertainment of travellers. It was near here the Israelites are believed to have crossed the Red Sea. A few miles

IN THE SUEZ CANAL.

distant, on an oasis in the Arabian Desert, are the brackish springs bearing the name of Moses, the largest of which tradition has marked as the one he called forth from the rock with his rod. Here, too, the treasures of Ophir were transshipped to Jerusalem and Tyre, and here, as well, the sands of two great continents greet each other in burning silence.

CHAPTER II.

ON TROPICAL SEAS.

> All are but parts of one stupendous whole,
> Whose body Nature is, and God the soul.
> POPE.

EARLY in the afternoon following our arrival at Suez, we received a hasty summons from the agent of the company to board the "Canara," as she was about to sail. In fifteen minutes we were steaming across the harbor in the launch, anxiously scanning the ship which was to be our moving home for nearly a month. Upon approaching her we were agreeably disappointed to find an almost new steamer, nearly three hundred feet long, and comfortably arranged, both on deck and below.

Our fellow-passengers, fifteen in number, all proved to be English except three. Four of them—three gentlemen and one lady—were bound for Zanzibar, as missionaries to the interior of Africa, sent by the two principal societies of London, representing the high and the low Church of England respectively.

Despite the hurry in bringing us on board, the ship never stirred until towards midnight, not an unusual experience for those who travel by the sea. However, in the interim we had abundant occupation in watching the embarkation of hundreds or thousands of pilgrims bound to Mecca. The steamers on which these devotees crowded like cattle were of the most inferior class, small, and having a worn aspect, as if age had withdrawn them from regular passenger traffic, or even from the better grade of freight service. When the period named by the Koranic law for the pilgrimage approaches,—the month of Zu'lheggeh, the last of the Muslim year,—these roving steamers, as well as many safer ones belonging to established lines, repair to various Mohammedan ports to secure assured cargoes of human freight. These they carry to Jeddah, about half-way down the Red Sea, the nearest point to the Holy City.

While daylight lasted the native boats continued their trips to the steamers, each bringing twenty or thirty men, until the decks were white with Arab gowns and turbans. Thus huddled together, many without the requisite supply of food, a voyage of four or five days is undertaken upon the most trying sea on earth. Afterward the same wretched herd must pass a month or more, amid deprivation and filth, in an unhealthy city, parched by the fierce sun of Arabia. Naturally enough, cholera broke out at Mecca. O Faith! thy chains are of iron strength, and thou canst work evil and misery, as well as deeds of good.

The ship had started, and the two lights, one red and one green, which mark the entrance to the Suez Canal, were disappearing in the distance before we went below for the night. Our long voyage, upon waters and to lands yet unseen by us, had actually commenced. Until now we had been traversing familiar ground; but henceforth, to the Golden Gate, a strange, new world promised to open before our expectant eyes its treasuries of sights and wonders.

Great was our regret when we learned that the "Canara" had been ordered to omit the usual calls at Jeddah, Hodeidah, and Mocha, because of the presence of cholera at those places and the subsequent quarantine entailed by visiting infected ports. In addition to this loss, the ship was ordered to be run at reduced speed to occupy the three days thus gained, that her schedule of dates might not be disarranged, even though we should be subjected to eight days of broiling in the fiery furnace of the Red Sea.

Slowly we descended the Gulf of Suez, with the rocky coast of Egypt on the right; and on the left, the sterile range of the Peninsula of Sinai, in the midst of which, during the first afternoon, we sought out the sacred mount from whose summit the God of Israel proclaimed the law unto Moses, and through him to the wandering children just freed from the house of bondage. Towards evening we entered the Red Sea proper. As yet we had suffered no inconvenience from the temperature, leading us to indulge the delusion that the famous heat had been exaggerated, or that, perhaps, we could escape it entirely at this particular season. Vain hope!

Morning dawned perceptibly warmer than any hour of the previous day, and when the sun neared the zenith the thermometer showed almost a hundred degrees beneath the double awnings covering both top and sides of the deck. The faint breeze, at first astern and later ahead, came as if from an oven. So it continued, day in and day out, moderating somewhat at night, until we passed out of this Red Hot Sea at the Gate of Tears, about a hundred miles from Aden. Even then the change was comparatively slight. But we were prepared for this fiery ordeal, and, as soon as it commenced, the remedies were applied. Underwear was discarded, and dark clothes gave way to suits of white duck or drill, with shoes to match, and the snowy helmet of India served to protect the head. Besides, thinking that conventionality would be a stranger on the Tigris and Euphrates, before leaving Suez we had our hair and beard clipped beyond the grasp of either comb or brush, a style of finish more simple than ornate.

Every night our beds were brought on deck, where we slept, fanned by the warm breezes and clad only in loose silk pajamas. At six in the morning the dark-skinned Lascars, the sailors of the Oriental lines, roused us to escape the approaching hose. While the decks were being deluged we went below for a sea-water bath, or promenaded shoeless and with the *caleçons* of the pajamas rolled up to the knees. Then came a cup of coffee and little strips of buttered toast, taken anywhere on deck beyond the momentary reach of the pursuing hose. That fiendish hose! I became so sensitive to its ominous splash as to hear it before awaking, sometimes starting up and grasping my bed to run with it before entirely conscious.

About eight o'clock it became absolutely necessary to endure the sweltering state-room long enough to slip into a white suit, buttoned up to the neck and without a collar of any kind. At nine came breakfast in the saloon, where the extreme heat was reduced by the swinging of the punka overhead. The punka, one of the institutions of India, is a long heavy wooden fan, usually with a pendant fringe of muslin or cloth, suspended from the ceiling and swung to and fro by a rope attached to its centre and extending through a hole to the hands of a coolie outside. The slender son of Asia who pulls this machine for hours at a time is called the *punka wallah*.

After breakfast we sought the shady side of the deck, and lounged upon our Indian chairs, reading or napping, until tiffin, or lunch, demanded renewed exertion. The chairs referred to are wholly unlike the folding ones used on trans-Atlantic steamers and much more comfortable, although not so portable. They are made entirely of bamboo, with the seat and reclining back close-plaited, long and permanent in form, with a foot-rest, broad arms, and receptacles for a tumbler and a handkerchief.

As soon as tiffin was disposed of the same lazy routine followed until the bell called us to dinner. When the opal tints in the west changed to gray, and the gray into night, the curtains around the deck were lifted, revealing the firmament spangled with a brilliancy unknown at home. Glittering, twinkling, darting, shining; the jewelled heavens above, the glistening waters beneath; a ship upon the sea, pilgrims on the voyage of life,—all! all! the wondrous mystery of creation, turning the thoughts to God. We walked and talked, pointed out the constellations, and struggled to be entertained by monotone music from the piano. Unfeigned was our joy when, between nine and ten, the ladies retired and the beds appeared, so that we could don our pajamas, and drift sweetly into the land of dreams, thinking of home and friends in our bereaved country beyond three seas. And then—that tormenting hose!

Having been forbidden to stop at Jeddah, the "Canara" proceeded down the middle of the sea, far away from the dangerous shoals and submarine coral reefs which fringe the shore, although we were frequently within sight of the barren, rocky, sandy, almost uninhabited coasts of Arabia, Nubia, and Abyssinia. It is from these parched desert tracts that the intense heat is exhaled over the deep blue waters. On the third day we passed the port for Medina, where the Prophet is buried; and farther south the officers indicated the location of

Jeddah by the rocks. Our disappointment at not being permitted to land there was aggravated by the knowledge that we should have seen the assemblage of pilgrims for Mecca, which is less than fifty miles distant, as it was but a fortnight to the first of the month of Zu'lheggeh. Unless the Mussulman enters the Holy City by that day his pilgrimage is void.

We also had a moderate feeling of curiosity to visit Eve's Tomb, which the Mohammedans have located at Jeddah, as the remains of the primitive mother are represented as having a length of three hundred and fifty feet. This shows that the ladies of her age must have been considerably taller than those of the present day, French heels included. With some regret I pass from Jeddah without describing the ceremonies of the pilgrimage, having already done so elsewhere.*

Some distance southward from Jeddah, on the Arabian shore, is Hodeidah, where we would have halted but for the cholera. Farther down we could almost discern Mocha, whence comes the choice coffee of that name. It was not until daylight of the seventh day that we passed through the Straits

---

* Outlying Europe and the Nearer Orient, chapter iv.

of Bab-el-Mandeb, or Gate of Tears, the entrance to which is commanded by the desolate, rocky island of Perim, situated in the channel between the two shores. Perim is held by England on account of its strategical value, and garrisoned by a single company from Aden. The British took possession of it only as late as 1865, upon accidentally hearing that two French men-of-war, then at Aden, were secretly bound on the same mission.

We anchored in the broad harbor of Aden before dawn on the eighth day, and rejoiced to be told that we might go ashore, as the ship was to remain four days. This privilege was unexpected, as cholera had just been epidemic and the port was still quarantined against as infected.

After sunrise the "Canara" was surrounded by small boats, and strange types of men boarded our decks. Parsees from Bombay, the fire-worshippers, with their peculiar tall Persian hats; Africans of the Somali nation, tall, slim, almost nude, and with moppy hair dyed a reddish color; Arabian Jews, the persistent venders of ostrich-feathers, for which Aden is the mart of the world, effeminate in face and manner, and wearing long side curls; Arabs, in summery attire and not unlike the Egyptians; a few Englishmen dressed in white, and enervated by the

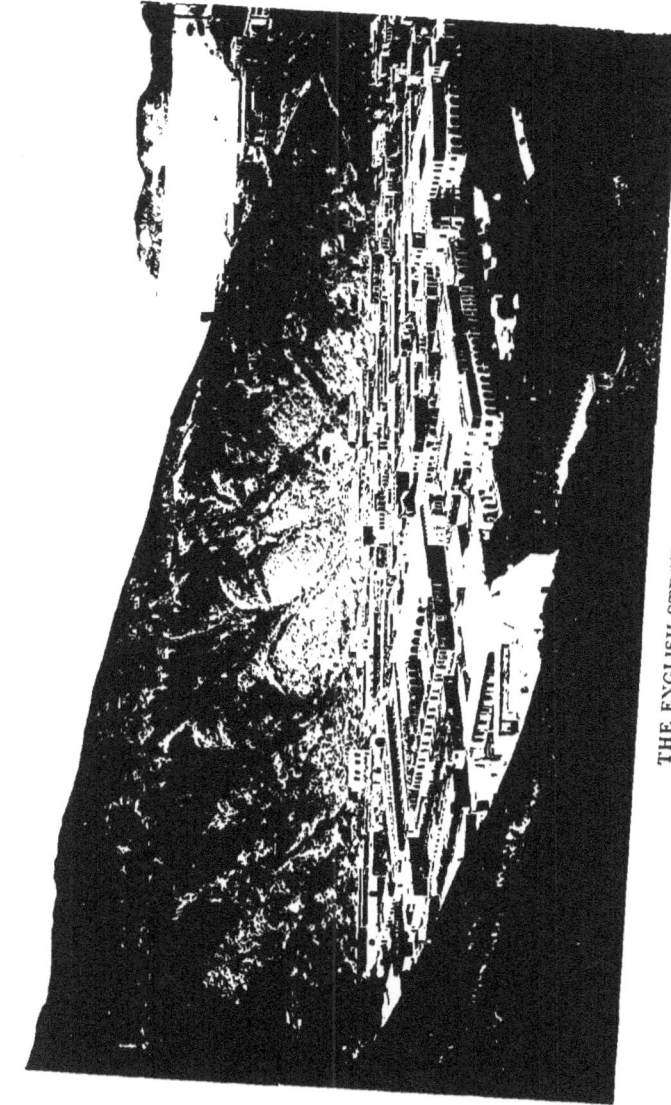

THE ENGLISH STRONGHOLD OF ADEN.

stifling summer climate; and the yelping, daring little diving boys, with only a rag about their loins, amphibious creatures who plunge for a coin with unerring success, or swim under the ship from one side to the other, or race around the buoys in their miniature dug-out canoes. Early each morning myriads of small sword-fish and bonitos gathered in the clear water about the steamer, and were easily taken with a line.

Upon landing we were beset by the people to buy, or accept a guide, or to drive in one of the several dilapidated extension-top American phaetons which have found their way here. The best shops for ostrich-feathers and curiosities are on the crescent facing the harbor, in what is known as Steamer Point, the town itself and the camp being across the narrow peninsula, and located, apparently, in the crater of an extinct volcano.

The entire promontory, which is strongly fortified and somewhat resembles Gibraltar, has a cindery aspect, and is utterly without vegetation. The solitary relief from this dreary monotony is a small artificial garden, with a few trees and plants, near the Tanks. Even this is sustained with great difficulty by a lavish expenditure of the precious water, which residents buy in skins at dear prices.

And yet there is a tradition among the Arabs that Aden is the site of the Garden of Eden!

The Aden of the present is but a shadow of the past, when it was a great commercial entrepôt on the highway between Europe and India. Of this former city nothing of importance is left except the famous tanks for the storage of water, which the English have repaired and brought into use. These works comprise a series of large reservoirs hewn out of the virgin rock, or partially formed by the addition of masonry, in a precipitous gorge above the town. As the rock is soft and full of cracks, the excavations have been lined with cement, to prevent the water from escaping. With these basins, although rain falls only at long intervals, a moderate supply of the vital liquid is generally maintained.

Of the origin of these tanks nothing definite is known. Some attribute them to colonists as early as the Phœnicians; but they were probably built in the flourishing period of the Arabians. Whatever may be their history, their conception, execution, and desertion serve to strengthen the moral pointed by the crumbling mounds of Nineveh and Babylon, by the stately ruins of Thebes and Palmyra, Athens and Rome, by the enlightenment of Occidental Europe, and by the rapid development of a mighty empire in America,—that, in the economy of Nature, the march of civilization and prosperity is steadily westward.

After spending four precious days lying in the broiling harbor of Aden, waiting for two passengers by the French mail steamer, the "Canara" finally sailed for Kurrachee. Before our departure a telegram had been received from London directing the ship to terminate her voyage at Kurrachee, instead of proceeding as usual up the Persian Gulf to Bussorah, on the Shat-el-Arab River. The reason for this order was the severe quarantine imposed at Ottoman ports against the cholera of India and the Red Sea, and the consequent delays and complications in handling freight and specie.

This change foreboded us trouble, as it implied a probable wait for the company's coastwise steamer, which consumes time by calling at several dull Gulf ports, and afterwards the sanitary detentions and failures to connect. So we left Aden feeling that our cherished expedition to Bagdad was in jeopardy, but still hopeful.

For three days after the bold promontory of Aden had disappeared in the distance we skirted the parched, rocky coast of Southern Arabia. On the fourth the barren panorama terminated with the

Kuria Muria Islands. Thence we headed across the Arabian Sea to Kurrachee, in the Indian province of Sindh, near the delta of the Indus, and close to the boundary of Beloochistan. The entire voyage of a week, save a single incident, was extremely monotonous, our daily routine resembling that on the Red Sea, except that the heat was more moderate.

The episode which alone varied the even current of our life on board was the death and burial of a young son of the lady and gentleman who joined us at Aden. Such an event, happening among a few closely thrown together, naturally cast its sombre shadow over all.

Although the boy was sick at the start, nothing serious was feared; but shortly pneumonia set in, and then it became evident that the bidden spirit was struggling to free itself from the weary body. The Hindu *ayah* flitted to and fro with anxious face; and the saddened mother fought for that little life as only a mother could. One evening, just after dinner, the end came unawares. The mother sat by her boy, but the childish soul was already voyaging on the arcane sea of eternity; upon "the mighty waters rolling evermore."

That night, when all was silent, they carried

up something rolled in white, and stowed it in one of the boats. Later, I stole a half-hour upon the bridge with the third officer, to enjoy the resplendent night. The tropical moon was at its full, and sea and sky reflected the glory of the Creator. We talked of the beauty about us and of the problems of navigation, but instinctively toned our voices so low that they seemed to harmonize with the profound stillness which reigned everywhere. Scarcely anything was said of the day's occurrence; but ever and anon our thoughts and our eyes turned to the boat which sheltered the dead, responsive to that strange, subtle influence attending the presence of death.

Early the following morning we gathered at the open rail, around a rude coffin shrouded with the Union Jack of England. The engine ceased its throbbing; the usual medley of noises was hushed, and the ship's bell tolled in mournful cadence.

"We therefore commit his body to the deep, to be turned into corruption, looking for the resurrection of the body (when the sea shall give up her dead) and the life of the world to come."

Down beneath the waves plunged the weighted box, to drift in the depths, from winter to summer, careless of sunshine or storm, until, perchance, the restless surf shall cast up

"A few white bones upon a lonely sand."

As we neared our destination it became almost certain that we would be a few hours late for the steamer from Bombay to the Gulf, involving a loss to us of six days. So slow was the speed of the "Canara," never exceeding nine knots, that the case was hopeless unless the company should detain the outgoing ship for our passengers, specie, and cargo.

We entered the harbor on a beautiful Sunday morning, and learned that the steamer had sailed the evening previous! Yet undaunted, we bade adieu to the gentlemanly officers of the "Canara," and went ashore to dispose ourselves for the enforced stay as favorably as circumstances would permit.

Only one of the two small hotels at Kurrachee was open, and that was full; so we took quarters at the Travellers' Bungalow. This hostelry, like most of those on the public roads of India, is a long, low structure of one story, with many doors but no windows, and sheltered from the sun by a veranda hung with curtains of matting. Within, the large apartments are almost bare of furniture, and in the rear of each is a rude out-house containing a round tub for bathing. The early coffee may be taken at will, but the breakfast at nine, tiffin at two, and dinner at eight are served in *table-d'hôte* style. Male servants alone are employed, and they are always addressed as "boys." The word bungalow, besides its use in the sense of a hotel, is also generally applied to the private houses of foreigners, whether they be in the cities or suburban.

Our efforts to talk with the servants in this bungalow produced at least one comical scene. Early in the morning, while we were still in our pajamas and I was lying upon the bare bed, my companion called the "boy," and undertook to order breakfast. The willing Hindu readily comprehended the word coffee, but neither signs nor repetition could make him grasp the idea of eggs.

While my friend was thus patiently struggling I could not resist the impulse to say "hen fruit." Its effect was electrical. The boy's face instantly brightened, and he exclaimed with evident relief, "Fruit! Yes, yes!" To remedy such a complication was a hopeless task, so we paid the penalty for the jest by having nothing more than bread and coffee, as the strange fruit was not to our taste.

Kurrachee is a straggling city of fifty thousand inhabitants and a seaport of some importance. In the cantonment, or new town, a few of the buildings are tasty, but the streets are horribly dusty and the sun grills the noonday pedestrian. The native quarter is a huddle of promiscuous humanity, naked or half clad, breathing an atmosphere which could be held accountable for any scourge. In the environs, on the sea-shore, is a bathing resort called Clifton, where huge turtles can easily be "turned" at daybreak. Kurrachee is also noted locally for its fish, of which the pomfret is the choicest.

About an hour's ride northward from the city, in a valley known as Magar Pir, the Hindus have located a temple on the borders of a swamp which swarms with alligators of the largest size. The place is dedicated to one of the many Brahmin deities, and pilgrims on their way to and from the shrine at Hinglaj make oblations of food to the sacred reptiles. If the offering is at once devoured, the omen is favorable; but, should satiety cause it to be declined, a liberal baksheesh will induce the obliging attendants to ram the mess down the holy monster's throat.

> "And ne'er did Faith with her smooth bandage bind
> Eyes more devoutly willing to be blind."

Two days after arriving in Kurrachee we received a visit from the captain of the "Canara," who brought with him the commander of the steamer bound southward from the Gulf ports. They kindly came to warn us that Bushire was prostrated by fever, and that the Turkish authorities at Bussorah would hold us ten days in quarantine on a barren, scorching isle below the city, among the sick and without the meanest necessities.

Further, by this delay we would miss the steamboat which ascends the Tigris to Bagdad, obliging us to pass another week in a mud town, "the dirtiest even in the Turkish dominions." What detention might follow on the downward trip, when the pilgrims from Mecca would be crowding homeward, or if the previous winter's plague should revive at Bagdad, could only be conjectured. Besides the risks of contagion, we clearly saw that to persist would involve the loss of so much time that our plans for the extreme East must be sacrificed.

For two hours we endured the mental struggle of indecision, battling with the inevitable. We were depressed, disappointed. In all the grand tour there was nothing we had been so ambitious to accomplish as this work upon the Tigris and the Euphrates, even though our reward should be little more than a gratification of sentiment: to stand upon crumbling mounds, amid silence and desolation, and traverse the deserted plains which once glittered with the pomp and splendor of Nineveh and Babylon. We were in earnest, and prepared for the task; but it seemed to be intended that we should turn aside. It was settled: we abandoned the project.

Until the facilities for travel improve, the journey through Asiatic Turkey and Persia should not be attempted in less than an entire autumn and winter. There are indications, however, that a sweeping change will soon be wrought in this inert section through the influence of the vast possessions which Russia and Great Britain have acquired in Asia. Schemes for a railway down the Valley of the Euphrates have already been discussed in England, and both Russia and Turkey are aiming for transcontinental lines to the gates of India.

When our resolution was taken, we made immediate preparations to leave for Bombay, and by sundown we were waving adieu to our quondam friends of the "Canara," as we steamed out of the harbor on the "Pachumba." And what a sight our ship presented! Between-decks were seventy horses of Persian and Arabian breeds, bound to the profitable market of India, and above she carried a motley assemblage of Orientals, numbering nearly three hundred. Among these passengers were about sixty men of the Fifteenth Bengal Infantry, just detached from the Quetta Column of the Anglo-Afghan war, then lately concluded, and returning to Calcutta. Their English officers, who were in the saloon, entertained us with recitals of the movements and hardships of that trying campaign.

Long before daylight on the third day we sighted the Prongs, or Colaba Light, and by dawn the ship was moored in the broad harbor of Bombay. We ran the gauntlet of the pestering natives and landed, feeling that *now* we were treading the soil of India. India! That "coral strand" of childhood too distant ever to be realized by the eye. But time works wonders, and here before us is India.

CHAPTER III.

BOMBAY.

Remark each anxious toil, each eager strife,
And watch the busy scenes of crowded life.
DR. JOHNSON.

BOMBAY seemed like a new world, despite its elements of similarity to Egypt or Asiatic Turkey. The people and their ways, the climate, the city itself, half beautiful and half miserable, are all different and strange. Even the landscape has its own tropical characteristics; the hills are dotted with groups of cocoanut-trees, as well as the white bungalows of the wealthy.

Then the carriages, or *gharries*, as they are called, are odd and novel. Fancy a gayly painted, diminutive cart, on two wheels, drawn by a pair of small trotting oxen, and filled with men or women dressed in the gaudiest colors; or a palanquin with latticed windows, as sombre as a Venetian gondola, and borne on a single pole by perspiring coolies. There is likewise a falling-top "buggy" on a pair

A STREET IN BOMBAY.

of wheels, with two seats for passengers and one in front for the native driver. Another vehicle is a narrow, enclosed box, with seats *vis-à-vis*, and hung low on four wheels. The hansom has also invaded Bombay, and the rich families drive on the Esplanade, or along the Breach Candy road, in the conventional London equipage, minus the gorgeous velvet coats and immaculate silk stockings of the august lackeys.

Nowhere had we seen clothing dispensed with to the degree witnessed here; and well it may be, as the climate is muggy and oppressive beyond all comparison. What it must be in summer is difficult to estimate, with such a winter. Winter, indeed! when one could scarcely exist in the gauziest raiment, aided by two baths daily. They told us it was *unusually warm* for the season. My companion lay awake three-fourths of the night, when there is not a breath of air stirring, and declared that everything is *unusual* wherever he goes. I managed somewhat better. I wrote, sweltered, and fought the mosquitoes until nature yielded, and sleep retained its sway until daylight.

Then the pandemonium of noises commenced; and as there were no bells, every one called "Boy! boy!" A host of utterly useless servants (the provoking, ubiquitous beggars!) held a carnival of jabbering, throwing about tin bathing-tubs, drawing water from pipes fed by a jerky pump, and running in and out of the rooms. Without waiting for an order, they knock at the doors and bring in coffee, and, if permitted, at once proceed to make the beds. We invited three of them out before seven one morning. Somewhat later we had the *dhobie* (laundryman), the *mehtar* (sweeper), a money-changer, a coolie with a box of purchases, and two bores,—one who wanted a situation as butler, and another who had a traveller's bed-quilt for sale. And then in walked the letter-carrier with our mail, according to the custom of his class.

The chief hotel is large and finely situated, but the service is wretched, the apartments untidy, the sanitary appointments very primitive, and the general effect disappointing.

But the climax of the servant farce is at meals. Then the dining-room swarms with "boys," many wearing the European livery of the house, and others the native costume, with huge turbans. The latter are privately employed, and each stands behind his master's chair. Think of the ornament and dignity they lend at the daily wages of only five annas, or less than fifteen cents! It should be stated, in extenuation, that the multiplication of servants so common in India is largely due to the demands of Hindu caste, which limits every man's sphere of labor. Of this subject, more in its place.

We drove through the bazaars, searching for Indian curiosities, and wondered at the throng of life everywhere. Brown skins almost nude, or else arrayed in snowy-white or fantastic colors, but always crowned with the bunchy turban, unless it be the peculiar tall, stiff hat of the Parsee. Hindus are easily distinguished from the Mohammedans by the stripes or round spots roughly painted on their foreheads, to indicate the caste to which they belong or the tutelary deity they specially worship.

The women are even more picturesque than the men. Decked in rainbow tints, with the garments drawn close to their undulating figures, they walk with firm and often graceful bearing. The nether limbs and feet are uncovered, and frequently the bust or waist will be partially exposed. They adorn themselves with a profusion of cheap bracelets of various materials, together with heavy anklets of silver, and a few rings find places on the toes. Earrings hang from the *top* of the ears, while one of the nostrils supports a ring or other ornament. If she happens to be a mother, the child is carried astraddle her hip.

Bombay is an island city, with one of the finest natural land-locked harbors on the globe. The lower, or English, section, called the Fort, occupies the site of a demolished citadel, and contains a group of surprisingly ornate and imposing public buildings, effectively spaced on broad avenues or on the Esplanade by the sea. In the native quarter we find the usual narrow streets of the Orient, unsavory odors, swarming humanity, and huddled, fanciful houses.

Here the bazaars, unlike those of Cairo, Damascus, and Stamboul, have no covering overhead, and prices are perceptibly higher than in those cities. The annoying system of bargaining, so universal in the East, prevails in Bombay, but not to the same extent we had heretofore experienced.

One of the many benefits of British rule in India has been to induce opulent natives to construct and endow public institutions; some from charitable motives, and others for the hope of distinction. To reward these acts of liberality, if they be of sufficient importance, the government confers the decoration of the Star of India, and, in exceptional cases, knighthood, or even a baronetcy. Thus the

THE NEW QUARTER OF BOMBAY.

surplus wealth of princes and merchants, instead of suffering waste in unneeded temples or extravagant tombs, as of old, is now gradually being directed into channels of education and utility.

In Bombay the Parsees are eminently conspicuous in these works, which accords with their status as the most progressive element of the population. Benevolent asylums, schools, colleges, fountains, and monuments have been raised, each tableted with the story of its creation, and bearing the complicated name of the donor. By frequently reading these inscriptions we soon become familiar with the good deeds of Sir Jamsetjee Jeejeebhoy, Bart., G.C.S.I., Sir Cowasjee Jeehangeer Readymoney, K.C.S.I., and Premchand Raichand, Esq., J.P.

The most curious of all the institutions of Bombay is the hospital which the Hindus have established for animals. Within the enclosure of several acres, located in one of the densest quarters of the city, the sick and the maimed of all domestic species are collected in sheds and stables for treatment or rest. Every morning early wagons are sent throughout the city to gather the outcasts and the waifs, that nothing with life may be destroyed, in violation of the Vedic law.

Birds as well as beasts are afforded shelter, not excluding repulsive vultures and scavenger crows. Dogs in every stage of scurvy, full of loathsome sores, barked and howled in distracting chorus as we passed their crowded cages. Cows and buffaloes of all sizes, old or diseased, and forlorn, bony horses, stood or lay in melancholy passiveness, as if patiently awaiting the relief of death. These, with helpless deserted kittens that must not be drowned, chickens with spots bare of feathers, monkeys scratching and tearing at their troubled hides, and perfumes not to be described, will afford some conception of this strange asylum.

A more alluring sight for a tropical winter morning is the Crawford Market, than which there is none finer anywhere. The buildings are of iron, airy in design and of great extent, surrounding a large gardened court. Fruit, vegetables, flowers, meat, spices, and fish are diligently tendered to all comers at the stalls, and a portion of the garden is allotted for the sale of poultry, birds of plumage, monkeys, and sometimes small animals, such as the mangoose.

After watching the natives bargain for flowers, to be placed in the temples as offerings, we inquired for the stands having the famous mangoes of Mazagon, a suburb of Bombay. This luscious though excessively sweet fruit was formerly so prized that Shah Jehan (1627) is said to have maintained a constant supply of it by relays of couriers from Delhi to the western coast, a stretch of nearly eight hundred miles. Here, in this bounteous mart, we also saw the leaf and nut of the betel, or areca palm, so generally chewed by the natives, blackening their teeth and giving the lips and saliva a reddish hue.

One afternoon of our sojourn at Bombay we are never likely to forget. Driving through the pretty suburbs to Malabar Point, and thence along the sea by Breach Candy, we ascended the hill and alighted at the road leading to the walled compound of the Parsee Towers of Silence. At the gate of the enclosure an officer required our permit, which was duly presented, signed by the Secretary of the Punchayat, or Committee of Five.

Full of curiosity concerning what we should be permitted to see, we were conducted with much deference to a low, heavy stone building—the house of prayer—as funereal in aspect as an old Etruscan tomb. Here we were asked to register our names in a book, after which a model of one of the towers was uncovered for inspection. We were then led through a garden and a grove of palms, the latter swarming with vultures and crows, to within about thirty feet of the largest of the five round towers. At this point our guide firmly indicated that no one was allowed to proceed farther, not even the most influential of the Parsees, excepting only the two bearded men who bear the remains after they are taken from the biers.

Upon gratings, on the summit of these towers, which are but twenty-five feet in height, the Parsees invariably expose the naked bodies of their dead. Scarcely a single hour elapses before every particle of flesh is devoured by the ravenous birds which ever haunt the locality. I counted thirty-five monster vultures quietly waiting on the great tower alone, which is nearly one hundred feet in diameter. On the slender palms they were crowding each other off the perches, snapping, or else fighting with their immense wings. It is estimated that a thousand of them are constantly present, not to mention a host of crows.

The bones either fall through into the well below, or are cast there, by the two gloved attendants, with tongs. After performing this duty they immediately purify themselves by washing and throwing away the white clothing always worn by those

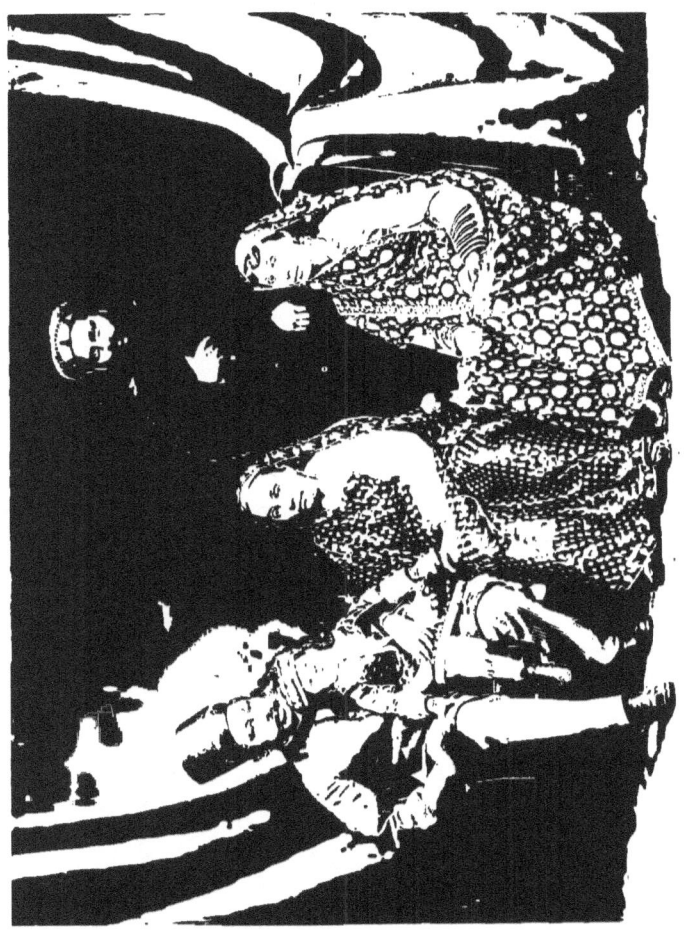

A PARSEE FAMILY.

participating in a funeral. This is done because a corpse is considered unclean,—an idea possibly borrowed from the ancient Egyptians. Those primeval devotees of Amun-Ra (the sun), like the Parsees for ages past, regarded the persons who handled the deceased as outcasts, and as such the unfortunates were condemned to live strictly among themselves.

The Parsees, who thus so uniquely reduce their dead, are followers of the philosopher Zoroaster,—the Ghebers, or Fire-Worshippers. They are of Persian descent, their early ancestors having been driven from Iran by the intolerance of the Muslim conquerors. By agreement with the Hindus, whose customs and religion they covenanted to respect, they were allowed to settle in Western India. Here, by their natural intelligence, progressiveness, and devotion to commerce, they have attained wealth, position, and influence.

Despite the prominent modern characteristics of the Parsees, they still adhere tenaciously to their original faith. Twenty-five centuries of thought and practice have wrought but little change in their creed. And when we consider that the same may be said of hundreds of millions of Hindus and Buddhists, what hope is there for regeneration in the future? The Parsees worship fire as the symbol of the Deity,—a shining light, the creator, dispenser, and preserver. In their Fire Temples, to which we were denied admittance, a flame is ever burning, fed with perfumed wood. Morning and evening the devout offer their prayers to the sun, not, as they claim, in idolatry, but in a vicarious sense, as the dazzling luminary is the most perfect visible evidence of the Divine presence.

In a note to "The Fire-Worshippers," in "Lalla Rookh," Moore quotes this extract: "Early in the morning they (the Parsees or Ghebers, at Oulam) go in crowds to pay their devotions to the sun, to which upon all the altars there are spheres consecrated, made by magic, resembling the circles of the sun; and when the sun rises, these orbs seem to be inflamed, and to turn round with a great noise. They have every one a censer in his hands, and offer incense to the sun."

This reverence for fire is also extended to the other elements. Hence the earth or the sea cannot be polluted with the dead. Even the rain which falls into the well of the funeral tower is disinfected by passing it through charcoal before it enters the drains. Yet, with all this pious care, it is evident that the air is defiled by their peculiar system.

Besides, an occasional bone drops from the talons of some repulsive bird into the city's reservoir near by, contaminating the water and exciting protests from other sects.

While we were yet upon the ground a funeral arrived,—fifty or more men all in white robes,—whereupon we were hurried away to the terrace adjoining the house of prayer. There we had a splendid view of Bombay and its environs; of the abodes of nearly three-quarters of a million of the living, many of whom are fated to be cast out as carrion.

Driving homeward by the route we had come, we witnessed yet another striking spectacle. Our carriage halted on the main road beside the gate of a long, high wall, where a sepoy invited us to enter. We did so, and after walking a few steps within the compound, or yard, the breeze came laden with a revolting stench. Noticing that we were about to retreat, our cicerone altered his course and guided us to a position outside the low rear wall of the enclosure, in a Muslim cemetery.

Here, just as night was falling, we climbed the wall, and found ourselves in the full glare of three Hindu funeral pyres. To the right of us the fires of as many more were about expiring. One directly in front of our perch, not over four or five yards distant, had been lighted only a few moments previously; and to that we directed our attention. We were now somewhat to the windward in the sea-breeze, which protected us from nauseating fumes, but not entirely from heat.

No furnace or retort of any kind is employed. A simple pile in the open air, not unlike a cord of wood in appearance, only about one-third smaller in dimensions, contains the corpse near the top. Four iron uprights driven into the ground prevent the logs from scattering. The torch is applied below, and the whole soon blazes and crackles. If a strong draft drives the flames away from either end, a portable iron screen is used as a fender. When the mass falls a few sticks are added, thoroughly to complete the cineration. A few friends of the deceased stand around, or coil themselves under a long shed, until all is finished.

The pyre immediately before us concealed the body of a man, but his long, bony feet and ankles protruded several inches. On the side towards us we could also see an emaciated hand. When the darting flames reached these extremities, and the brown skin first blistered and withered and then peeled, the broiling, dripping flesh was a ghastly sight. Still we held our places. As the cremation

A HINDU BURNING-PLACE.

progressed the mourners were apparently more amused than impressed, as they repeatedly smiled when one part after another was consumed. In less than an hour all visible portions of the remains were charred, and the pile showed indications of tumbling. Having already seen adjacent pyres in the remaining stages of the process, we gladly exchanged our tiresome place on the wall for the more comfortable gharry.

As we drove homeward and reviewed the memorable experiences of the day, I thought of the horrible scenes which must have been enacted in Hindu crematories when living women burned themselves with their dead husbands. Little as British policy cares to interfere with the religious observances of its Indian subjects, humanity and civilization long ago successfully demanded the abolition of sutteeism. The same progressive edict likewise stopped the dread wheels of Juggernaut's car, crushed the murderous Thugs, and arrested the arm of the fanatical mother bent upon throwing her infant to the crocodiles of the Ganges.

In contrasting these two expeditious methods of disposing of the dead, the enlightened mind will quickly decide in favor of that of the Hindu. But the great objection to their mode is its crudeness.

If they could be induced to adopt the plan of sealing the body in a retort, somewhere removed from the populous highways, much might be urged in defence of their system. In the climate of India the decomposition of lifeless animal matter is rapid and pernicious, and the people live in utter ignorance of sanitary precautions. Our only wonder is that sweeping epidemics of cholera, smallpox, and fever are not more frequent. Fire at once obviates the danger of contagion or of shallow burial.

Again, the large mortality in a population of two hundred and fifty millions, constantly accumulating, would require an enormous area for cemeteries; removing from the sphere of production much valuable ground in the vicinity of cities, towns, and villages. Constantinople, for example, is fairly encircled with dreary sepulchres, in all degrees of neglect and decay.

One of the denizens of the streets of Bombay, as well as of Cairo, is the snake-charmer. He haunts the locality of the larger hotels, and persuades travellers in a begging, wheedling manner to spare just a few moments for his little entertainment. The instant he secures the coveted attention a formidable cobra, about four feet in length, lazily

SNAKE CHARMERS.

uncoils itself from a round basket and wanders over the ground. Sometimes it will be a rock snake, or boa, of nearly double the size named; but this species is innocent of the deadly fangs of the former. Next, perhaps, he liberates a hooded cobra, and then two or three harmless grass snakes, which wriggle away so rapidly that they almost escape. The charmer gathers the small reptiles in one hand, and with the other twines the cobra around his neck or waist. Although he pretends to guard against being touched by the fatal venom, we were sceptical enough to believe that the docile captive had been deprived of its fangs.

A mangoose is now produced,—a little animal resembling a weasel, and to which the bite of a serpent is said to be innocuous. One of the small snakes, upon being thrown down, was wickedly attacked by the diminutive creature and so savagely bitten about the head that it soon became limp and covered with blood.

The snakes are finally thrust into the baskets and the usual tricks follow. One of them, at least, is worthy a description. In the hemisphere of a cocoanut shell filled with water the conjurer placed a painted toy duck. This simple apparatus stood on the ground directly before us, and removed from all other objects. Retiring to the distance of a yard or more, the man played upon a native drum, and the tiny duck responded by dancing in unison with every beat. We offered the juggler a sovereign for the secret, but he declined with a salaam and left with his modest baksheesh.

We devoted one of our last days in Bombay to visiting the celebrated rock temples known as the Caves of Elephanta. The island of that title, which contains these remarkable excavations, is situated in the harbor, about six miles from the city. Its name is derived from a colossal stone elephant, dating from the tenth century, the remains of which are near a former landing. The sail across the bay was full of variety, and afforded an opportunity to see the antiquated native boats. Moored in the channel was one of the monster British troop-ships which convey the home contingent to and from India.

The principal temple at Elephanta consists of a large main chamber and two lateral wings, all hewn out of the virgin porphyry rock in the hill-side. Massive pillars, crowned with fluted, cushion-like capitals, support the lofty ceiling. In the centre, at the end of the hall, is the Trimurti, or three-faced image of the Hindu Trinity, — Brahma,

THE CAVES OF ELEPHANTA.

Vishnu, and Siva,—the Creator, the Preserver, and the Destroyer. These effigies are gigantic in size and immobile in countenance.

At the side, in the central cavern, is an adytum containing the Ling stone, a low, cylindroid post with a rounded head. This is worshipped as a representation of Siva's power over nature. The walls of the temple are carved with archaic high reliefs, in panels, picturing the marriage of Siva and Parvati; Ravunu, the demon king of Ceylon, attempting to steal Kylas, or the heavenly hill; and other mythical subjects.

The origin of these caves is unknown, but they are supposed to have been executed between the eighth and twelfth centuries of our era. Many similar ones exist in different parts of the Peninsula, particularly in the south. They are more imposing than the excavations at Beni-Hassan, but suffer when compared with the stupendous Temple of Aboo-Simbel, the creation of the mighty Rameses.

CHAPTER IV.

ACROSS INDIA BY RAIL.

So we see that nations are changed by time; they flourish and decay; by turns command, and in their turns obey.—OVID.

So uncomfortable and oppressive was the weather in Bombay that it was a relief when the evening came for our start inland. As few of the hotels in India supply more than the *charpoy*, or native wooden bedstead, for sleeping, we provided ourselves with pillows and *resais*,—quilted coverlets. These, with the rugs we already had, made huge bundles, such as would excite a smile in Europe or America. Here everybody travels with these comforters, and hence their bright colors and cumbrous bulk are not in the slightest conspicuous. On the road, too, they are indispensable for warmth, as the winter nights are piercingly cold on the vast plateau which stretches from the Ghauts, or coast range, to the Himalayas.

As the distances are long and the pace slow, in traversing India many a night must be passed on the train. To meet the want which this creates, the first-class carriages, and most of the second, are furnished with seats like sofas, with a folding, hanging couch above on each side. Every compartment, for either four or six passengers, has a small toilet attached. An abundance of water is supplied, but no towels or soap. The latter, however, is no deprivation after one becomes accustomed to the more cleanly habit of carrying those essentials.

I wonder that some disciple of Frith has never pictured the scene in an Indian station before the departure of a train. Few studies could be more prolific of life, novelty, and action. It is babel, excitement, and din. The natives are fond of travel, and scores collect hours before they can hope to take their places. When the doors are opened they instantly crowd the long string of third-class carriages, hurrying to and fro with their effects, chattering, shouting, and wrangling.

Nothing like work is ever done without noise, and upon so rare an occasion their lungs are taxed to the utmost. Frequently a dozen friends will come to say adieu to one person, and many throng the platforms from mere curiosity. To these simple creatures—for they are more like children than men and women—all that pertains to railroading is a toy of which they never tire.

When a gharry arrives with *sahibs*, as Europeans are called, the coolies gather as "numerous as gnats upon the evening gleam." If permitted, three or four of these parasites will fasten themselves to each trunk, and as many more to the hand luggage. No matter how slight their claim may be, they follow a traveller with both palms extended, clamoring for baksheesh. They are rarely content with a tip, be it generous or otherwise. Reasoning with them is a waste of time, and forbearance almost a useless virtue. According to the experience of old Anglo-Indians, the average native respects only power and word of command.

We chose the new line to the interior,—the Bombay, Baroda, and Central India,—as it would enable us to visit a section recently opened to travel, and to avoid doubling upon our tracks for a considerable distance. Besides, the old route by Jubbulpoor offers little of interest from Bombay to Allahabad, a sweep of nearly a thousand miles.

The day was waning as the train passed through the pretty suburban railway stations, all twined with flowering vines, and along the shore by the blue waters, now glowing with the blazonry of sunset. After dark we crossed a succession of bridges, some of notable length, which span the many rivers whose embouchures here indent the sea. Although we had glimpses of the Ghauts in the east, the landscape in general was of the monotonous jungle type. At midnight the train reached Surat, the cotton entrepôt of India, where we alighted, hungry and dusty.

Shrine of the mighty! Is this the porter? A woman! First one, then two, three, four, grasped the luggage and bore it on their heads to the buffet, thoughtless of the uncovered busts which their elevated arms brought into bold relief. Two pairs of these shoeless Amazons went forward to the van and returned with our trunks, both as heavy as lead, upon their heads, yet without unusual exertion. We looked about for coolies, but none could be seen; we were in the territory of the stanch "carrying women" of Surat.

The rooms at the station, which we had been recommended to occupy, were simply not to be endured; so we hired a two-wheeled bullock-cart, and trotted across the city to the dawk (travellers') bungalow, pleasantly located near the river Taptee, where we found tolerable quarters.

Before we left our rooms next morning the

"merchants" were peering into the windows, eager to sell the wood-work, inlaid with ivory and metal, for which Surat is famous. After breakfast the manager of the bungalow, an educated native, or baboo, sent for a covered bullock-cart. The gharry-wallah, or driver, of this novel equipage proudly declared that his team, a neat pair of dove-colored oxen, could beat any on the road. Be that as it may, we certainly had no reason to complain of the service they rendered us during the day.

Surat is the capital of an extended collectorate, and shelters in itself above a hundred thousand inhabitants. Formerly the pilgrims from all parts of Hindustan embarked for Mecca at this port. The prosperity of the city caused it to fall a prey to the Portuguese early in the sixteenth century, and at the beginning of the seventeenth the first English factory was established. Soon after the Mogul Emperors granted the same privilege, first to the Dutch and then to the French. Less than a century ago Surat claimed a population of three-quarters of a million; but repeated disastrous floods of the Taptee and a destructive conflagration in 1837 have reduced it to its present estate.

Cotton is the paramount interest of the section which recognizes Surat as its centre, and the city

AN INDIAN EQUIPAGE.

contains three or four manufactories of moderate capacity. We visited the mills of the Jafur Alee Spinning and Weaving Company, where the Scotch manager received us most hospitably and conducted us through every department without reserve. The product of the concern is chiefly unbleached cloths and sheeting.

Although the process developed nothing that would be new to our home spinners, the hundreds of native operatives could not be classed in the same category. They comprised Hindus and Muslims of all ages and both sexes. Many are skilled at their tasks, as the manager proved by breaking threads and in other ways requiring nimble fingers to remedy disorder. Labor is compensated by the piece, at extremely low rates. Work as she will, a woman cannot earn above five annas (about fourteen cents) a day, and the best loom hand not more than eight, or less than a "quarter." Think of it, ye thrice-blessed toilers of America, and be content.

The unassuming Scotchman frankly admitted that Surat cottons would not compare with the finer grades of American growth, nor could they compete with ours in the London market. During the Rebellion, when the Southern ports were blockaded, the cultivation of cotton and its manufacture received an undue impetus in Western India. An immense area was planted, mills were built, and speculation became rampant. When Richmond fell a panic ensued. Cotton property collapsed, enterprises were wrecked, and traffic stagnated. Wealthy Anglo-Indians and the Parsee capitalists of Bombay were the principal sufferers. A partial revival has since occurred, placing the trade on a normal basis and enabling several of the factories to resume work at a profit.

The bazaars of Surat proved commonplace, and we saw little that was striking in architecture, excepting perhaps the sombre Castle. One curious sight, however, was an old English cemetery, with many quaint epitaphs and a cluster of mausoleums designed like mosques and heathen temples. Here is an example of one of the inscriptions:

"In memory of Mary Price, wife of William Price, Esq., chief for affairs of the British Nation, and Governor of the Mogul Castle and fleet of Surat, who, through the spotted veil of the small-pox, rendered a pure and unspotted soul to God, experiencing death, which ended her days April the 13th. Anno Domini 1761. Ætatis Suæ 23.

"The virtues which in her short life were shown
Have equal'd been by few, surpass'd by none."

Another relates that the departed "went unmar-

A SWEETMEAT SHOP OF SURAT.

ried to the heavenly nuptials, in the year of Christ, 1649," and in a third instance a tablet records the span of a very brief life:

"Here lies the body of the infant child of Major Charles and Martha Frederick, born at 10 o'clock at night on the 29 of September 1786 and died at 3 o'clock the next morning, God rest her soul."

During the afternoon, while in the bazaars, we met a long procession headed by a portion of the garrison band, together with men and boys playing reed instruments and beating drums in shrill discord. After them came a string of people of both sexes, arrayed in holiday attire; and following these a troupe of singers preceded the bearers of banners and shrines lavishly decked with tinsel. Succeeding this group was a boy, gaudily dressed and numerously attended, riding a pony caparisoned in the most extravagant manner. The remainder of the line consisted of carriages of every style, and most of them without occupants. This noisy pageant, we learned, was a part of the festivities of a Hindu wedding.

While driving across the city the previous night we had noticed an illumination in one of the larger houses, although the hour was so late. This proved to be the residence of the two brides, the sister daughters of "a rich Hindu with twenty thousand rupees (about eight thousand five hundred dollars, nominally ten thousand dollars) a year." The girls were respectively about seven and eight years of age, and the bridegrooms slightly their seniors. After the conclusion of the festival, which may continue for a week, the wedded couple return separately to their parents' homes, there to abide until puberty. Then the husband, a boy of thirteen or fourteen years, goes in gaudy state to claim his wife.

The nuptial ceremony of the Hindus is performed by one or more Brahmins, and is very tedious, occupying several hours. It concludes by joining the hands of the affianced with a sacred cord, and repeating certain texts. These childish marriages are, of course, arranged by the parents; and lacking, as they do, the cardinal principle of free and mature choice, they frequently lead to anything but happiness. Large sums are expended upon the lengthy fête by which this social event is celebrated, every man striving according to his means to outdo his townsmen.

In the evening, after dinner, the manager of the bungalow sent for a bevy of Nautch girls, who came accompanied by two musicians. Strangely enough, two of them proved to be members of a band lately exhibited in New York. Having been told that they were to appear before American sahibs, they brought photographs of themselves by metropolitan artists, which they handed us with great delight. With the baboo as interpreter, we heard the story of their experiences in the New World. The cold winter had caused them much suffering, and one of their number died. They earned comparatively little, having contracted for only a small monthly stipend; but the more experienced lessees had profited by their services.

Having donned their finery in a rear apartment, the entertainment began. The costume, which concealed the entire figure, was of light materials in various colors and much ornamented with gold lace. Jingling anklets of silver, bracelets, and rings in the ears and nose constituted the jewelry. The dance, if such it can be called, was as disappointing as that of the Egyptian Ghawazee; and the songs by which it is accompanied were shrill and monotonous. The movements are simply a series of postures, repeated over and over again.

After the fantasia one of the group prepared the leaf and nut of the betel, with lime and spices, and invited us to chew one. This we were obliged to decline, much to their regret. The youngest of the girls had some pretensions to beauty, which probably led to the adoption of her degrading profession, for the Nautch girls are the lost ones of India.

Everywhere on the streets of Surat, as in other cities, the sepoys, or native police and soldiers, were perpetually saluting us *à la militaire*. This mark of deference to European sahibs is not uncommon throughout India, but our taut patrol jackets of duck and white helmets, likening us to British officers, caused a perceptible increase of the attention. Often squads on duty, at gates or police stations, seized their pieces and formed to present as our carriage passed. Guards before government buildings and sentries on the parapets rarely omitted to bring the musket to a shoulder, and galloping cavalrymen held themselves erect and stretched out the arm and hand from the saddle.

At first it was a novel and amusing duty to respond to these salutations twenty or thirty times a day, but later I carried my hand to the helmet like a veteran of the Mutiny. And if an occasional high private neglected this recognition of my mystic rank, I quenched any slight irritation by

NAUTCH GIRLS.

the thought that the heathen's training was sadly deficient.

This ostentatious reverence for Europeans is also displayed by the mass of the people,—in the bazaars, on the highways, and about the hotels. Servants coiled upon the floors of the corridors or on the porches rose to salaam, almost bending double, as we approached. When we drove, our Jehus impudently demanded, and were meekly granted, the right of way by wagons of burden, heavily-laden elephants, camels, or oxen, no matter in which direction we might be proceeding. On the streets or in the shops old men and young, women, and even little children, bowed the head and crooked the back in token of inferiority.

But I have no faith in the sincerity of this willing abasement; it is the treacherous humility which "licks yet loathes the hand that waves the sword." Perhaps the future will explain the growing power of the Caucasian in Asia by the stern law of the survival of the fittest; by a repetition of the plaintive history of the American Indian.

We arrived in Surat at midnight, and took our departure at the same uncomfortable hour. When our bullock-cart reached the station the tireless "carrying women" again took our weighty trunks upon their heads, and bore them up a flight of steps to the platform. We walked almost beside them, encumbered only with a sun umbrella.

An anomaly indeed; but in many things the East reverses the manners and customs of the West. In the former men remove their shoes instead of the head-covering when entering houses and holy places; women suspend their ear-rings from the top of the ear; Persian-Arabic is read backward, from the last to the first page of a book. We are enjoined to keep the head cool and the feet warm; but the Oriental wraps his precious cranium with twenty or thirty yards of muslin, and goes without a rag from the knee downwards. If a man and his wife journey to the city with one beast, he gallantly rides, while she dutifully trudges in the rear with the baby or a great bundle.

We crossed the river Nerbudda by a bridge nearly a mile long, and hurried through Broach without halting for the sport we were recommended to enjoy there. Our English cousins are wedded to the shot-gun and the rifle, and many of them come to India and travel about the world mainly "to do a bit of shooting." Early in the morning we had coffee at Baroda, and went on to Ahmedabad for breakfast. We afterwards regretted not having spent a day at the latter city, once the metropolis of Western India. It possesses the finest example of pierced marble screen-work to be found in the Peninsula, and several pieces of architecture much extolled by Fergusson.

After passing Mount Aboo, the seat of a group of Jain shrines, we saw numbers of wild monkeys, or apes, and myriads of birds, large and small. Ajmere was lost to view in the darkness, and daylight was upon us before we alighted at Jeyporo, our destination. The trap which conveyed us from the station to the travellers' bungalow was a marvel,—the shrunken ponies, the narrow box on wheels, and the skeleton driver. When it started on a gallop everything rattled and creaked, and a crash threatened at every moment. The trunks on top added to the general unsteadiness, yet a corner was turned so recklessly that we barely escaped upsetting. It was no little relief to be landed at our quarters without accident, where we firmly declined a proffer of the same conveyance to see the city.

The Rajpoots, literally the "sons of kings," are a martial people, and proudly claim to be descendants of the ancient royal Kshatriyas, or warrior caste of India. Their province, Rajpootana, which is now under British protection, is divided into eighteen principalities, each having its own ruler and many lesser chieftains. Jeypore, the capital of one of these modest States, is picturesque and essentially of Indian aspect, yet it bears the marks of the progressive character of its princes. Until early in the last century the seat of government was at Ambher, four miles from Jeypore; but owing to a prophecy of the Brahmins, that it would bring disaster if his line reigned more than a thousand years in one place, the superstitious Rajah Jey Sing built the present city and removed his court.

Having yielded to the priestly fiction, the otherwise sensible monarch determined that his new capital should be a model in design and construction. As a result, we see broad streets, intersecting at right angles, regular blocks of houses, open squares, and a grand public garden. His successors, not less modern in their secular ideas, have improved the drainage, introduced gas, beautified the garden, and added the water-works. Among the municipal institutions are a college, library, museum, and school of arts. We were conducted through the last named, and found much entertainment in watching the artisans engaged upon objects for an exhibition at Calcutta.

Although Jeypore combines the elements of a

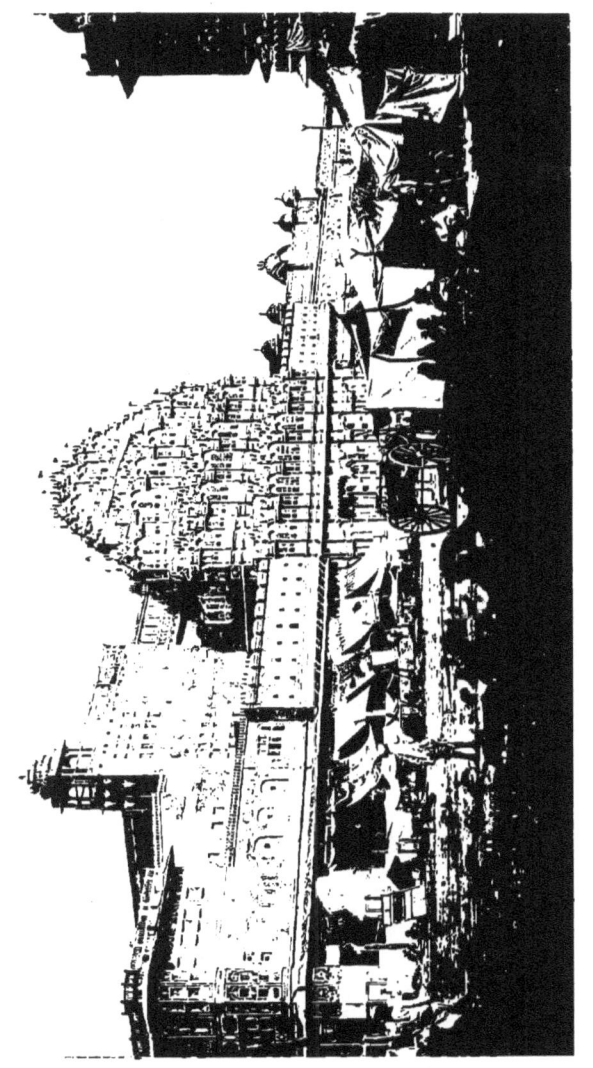

WIND PALACE AND BAZAAR, JEYPORE.

striking picture, its architecture is somewhat monotonous and seldom imposing. Its defect arises from too great a similarity of outline, the absence of lofty structures, and the universal use of pink distemper for mural ornament. The palace stands nearly in the centre of the city, and, with its gardens, covers about one-seventh of the space within the walls.

Excepting the Hall of Audience, or throne room, which is of marble, and a curious astronomical observatory, there is little of note about this tawdry pile. Adjacent to it, and fronting on a wide avenue, is a whimsical summer residence known as the Palace of the Winds. The pink façade is a mass of miniature bay-windows, glazed with small panes,—a faint suggestion of the Palace Hotel of San Francisco.

In the same vicinity are the royal stables, an immense quadrangle of sheds with a commanding tower attached. Here we had the pleasure of seeing the youthful Maharajah, who was seated upon a dais and giving directions about the harness and carriages which had been brought for his inspection. Owing to the presence of the sovereign, the gatekeeper had denied us admission to the enclosure; but at the suggestion of the guide we sent our cards to the Maharajah, who courteously invited us to enter. As we passed near where he sat he saluted us politely. The official who attended us stated that the stables contain three hundred horses, chiefly Persian and Arabian stock. In addition to the halter, it is customary to secure a horse with a rope to each heel.

The main thoroughfare of the city, extending from the Gate of the Moon to the Gate of the Sun, is a kaleidoscope of Indian life. Both sides are flanked with the usual diminutive Oriental shops, raised about a yard above the ground and shaded by little awnings. Natives of all castes, and rarely a European, throng the innovating pavements, many with swords at the waist and shields strapped low down the back, or with long matchlocks slung over the shoulder. The rich dyes of Rajpootana are displayed in the costumes met at every step; the wearers flitting hither and thither, or standing in knots, or sitting upon the floors of their business places.

In the dusty streetway huge elephants lumber along, spirited stallions gallop past, gharries dash up and down, coolies plod by with palankeens, and strings of camels wend their way through the maze. Among the concourse we may distinguish a mounted Thakur, or nobleman from the districts, accompanied by his barbaric men-at-arms. Order prevails, and the people are peacefully following their pursuits.

Wherever we alighted from the carriage groups of annoying but respectful natives collected, brimming with curiosity to see us bargaining for Rajpoot weapons, indigenous garnets and carbuncles, or spangled slippers with curled toes. When the difference between the buyer and the seller rendered a trade doubtful, these grown children, unable to refrain, interposed their advice and chattered with the zeal of an interested party. At this juncture the guide would sharply command the whole assemblage to leave, whereupon they meekly dispersed, like a canine with his expressive appendage in the attitude of bodily fear.

Led by the baboo, we penetrated a narrow, repulsive alley and entered the wretched dens where the Hindu gods are carved in marble. This industry is one of the specialties of Jeypore, and considerable archaic skill is evinced in the workmanship. In addition to small specimens of the deities, we bought effective models of elephants bearing finely-colored howdahs, and little figures in hard black stone.

We gave an afternoon to Ambher, the deserted capital, and drove slowly among its decaying buildings. Many are yet in a fair state of preservation. The city is located in a valley surrounded on all sides by rocky hills.

At the foot of the road leading to the Citadel we found one of the Maharajah's elephants, which had been kindly placed at our disposal by previous appointment. At a signal from his driver, who was perched upon his neck, the mighty beast went down on his knees, and then, by means of a ladder, we climbed to the howdah on his back. When he rose the sensation was not one of absolute security, but we managed to retain our places through the unsettling movement, and off he marched. Despite his formidable proportions he proved steady and docile, depositing us safely at our elevated destination in less than an hour.

The view from the Citadel up the valley, overlooking a lake, the temples and mosques of the city, and the beautiful landscape beyond, alone repaid for the expedition. We wandered through the vast, uninhabited palace, but discovered nothing specially attractive, except a few examples of perforated marble screens and the glass apartments. The walls and ceilings of the latter are veneered

THE DESERTED CITY OF AMBHER.

with thousands of small mirrors, arrayed in a variety of designs.

Destruction hovers over temple and citadel, palace and city, certain of its prey. Superstition, under the guise of religion, has doomed all this fair creation to deliberate waste; but the Nemesis of Nature's offended laws is already visiting the generations of those guilty of this prodigal crime.

CHAPTER V.

CITIES OF THE MOGULS.

> High lifted up were many lofty towers,
> And goodly galleries far over laid,
> Full of fair windows and delightful bowers.
>
> SPENSER.

ONE sweep to the northeast from Jeypore brought us to Delhi, the capital of the extinct Mogul Empire, the Mecca of the East. What a train of thought is suggested by its very name! With a history dating back to the mythical period of the early Aryans, it was destroyed seven times and as often rose again to dominion and grandeur.

Here the Pathans of Ghuzni, under Mohammed Ghory, founded (A.D. 1193) the Muslim empire of India; and two centuries later (1398) the ruthless Tamerlane came with his fanatical hordes to burn, plunder, and drench the streets with blood. Next the Sultan Baber, the descendant of Zinghis Khan and Tamerlane, crossed the Indus and established the Mogul throne (1526) in the conquered city.

THE GREAT MOGULS.

This memorable dynasty "continued to flourish with only one interruption, and with increasing lustre, for a hundred and eighty years, under a succession unprecedented in Indian history, of six sovereigns, distinguished by their gallantry in the field, and, with one exception, by their ability in the cabinet."

This galaxy of successful, though cruelly rapacious and utterly unprincipled rulers, consists of Baber, Humayoon, Akbar, Jehangeer, Shah Jehan, and Aurungzebe. About these names cluster the relics of the power and splendor of the Great Moguls, the superb monuments of dazzling extravagance by which travellers are chiefly drawn to the imperial seats of Delhi and Agra.

Modern Delhi is the work of the Emperor Shah Jehan (1627–1658), a monarch celebrated for the splendor of his tastes, for the order of his finances, and for his love of building. As the new city approached completion he left Agra, whither the great Akbar had removed his court, and Delhi again became the Mogul capital.

The Fort, or citadel,—which contains the palace, now partly destroyed, the exquisite marble gem known as the Pearl Mosque, the luxurious baths, and the lavish pavilions of state,—is the finest in

India. Its gateways are in themselves imposing structures, and the lofty castellated walls of red sandstone describe a circuit of more than a mile. Within the enclosure of the city are the famous Shalimar Gardens, now called the Queen's, beyond which the inmates of the zenana, or harem, never passed.

The culmination of all this magnificence is reached in the Dewan-i-Khas, or Hall of Private Audience, which overlooks the river Jumna and the plain. This edifice is of marble, open at the sides and supported by massive square columns, the whole being adorned with mosaics of costly stones and inlaid gold. Adjoining it are the private apartments of the sovereign, where the pierced marble screens, wrought in floral designs, are of startling richness.

In this hall stood the renowned Peacock Throne, which was plundered by the Persians, a mass of solid gold flanked by two peacocks, with distended tails, all studded with diamonds and rubies, sapphires, emeralds, and pearls. The value of this wonder was estimated at six crores, or sixty millions of rupees, nominally thirty million dollars. On the cornices of the marble platform which bore the throne is the Persian inscription which Thomas

HALL OF PRIVATE AUDIENCE, DELHI.

Moore introduced so effectively in "The Light of the Harem":

> "If there be an Elysium on earth,
> It is this, it is this."

Shah Jehan was not long permitted to enjoy the grandeur he had created. During an illness which brought him to the point of death, his four sons became involved in a bitter conflict for the succession; and so far had it been carried by the time of his recovery that he was unable to resume his authority. The bold and subtle Aurungzebe overpowered all resistance, dethroned his father, and imprisoned the fallen monarch in the fort at Agra. There he spent the remaining seven years of his life, within sight of that sublime mausoleum, the Taj, which he had reared to the memory of the adored wife of his youth.

Despite this heartless act, to which he added the death of his brothers, Aurungzebe lived to reign almost half a century (1658–1707), and to wage a war of intolerance for twenty-five years. But the close of his career was tortured by suspicion, gloom, and remorse, and after his death the strained empire began to decline.

Lalla Rookh was the daughter of this cruel

prince, and it was from the gate of the Fort already noticed that she set out upon the journey to meet her future husband in the Vale of Cashmere.

The day of her "departure from Delhi was as splendid as sunshine and pageantry could make it. The bazaars and baths were all covered with the richest tapestry, hundreds of gilded barges upon the Jumna floated with their banners shining in the water, while through the streets groups of beautiful children went strewing the most delicious flowers around; and as Aurungzebe stood to take a last look from his balcony, the procession moved slowly on the road to Lahore."

Although Ireland's "sweetest lyrist" never visited the East, the scene he pictures may have been enacted at Delhi a century before his generation. But if his studies of forgotten writers have not prompted him to exaggerate, as in many instances, how completely has everything changed! Not a shred of the pomp he sketches is now to be seen.

Even the Chadney Chook, the once famous thoroughfare and bazaar, has lost its lustre, and apparently every honest merchant it ever possessed. Mendacity is there a commercial virtue and cheating legitimate business tact. Taking them as a class, they are the most treacherous body of traders we

THE GREAT BAZAAR OF DELHI.

ever encountered. In view of these characteristics, our shopping was done with the greatest difficulty. At the hotel, a wretched hostelry, and in the Chadney Chook, travellers are constantly annoyed by having cards thrust at them, accompanied with pressing invitations to call.

Conspicuous among the wares thus so diligently offered are cashmere or "India" shawls, and white Rampoor chudders, a similar wrap for head and body. The latter are made of the fine wool of the Himalaya goat, and often so delicate and sheer that they can be drawn through a finger-ring. Gold and silver embroidery is also a specialty of Delhi, as well as miniatures painted on ivory, and Indian jewelry of the usual barbaric designs.

While the Chadney Chook has parted with its former glitter, there is much in its present throng of life to attract the searcher after novelties. Picture, for instance, a semi-European carriage bearing four servants in gaudy Oriental livery and drawn by a pair of trotting dromedaries. The ordinary conveyance is the picturesque little *bali*, an ox-cart furnished with a cushion and a red canopy, under which the higher-grade native female coils herself, secure from the public gaze. Another common vehicle is a simple board, sometimes with a covering overhead, slung by four ropes to a pole and borne by two coolies.

The last vague shadow of the Mogul dynasty,

> "That saintly, murderous brood,
> To carnage and the Koran given,"

vanished in the great Sepoy Mutiny (1857); but Delhi is yet the revered centre of the forty millions of Muslims in India. Their cathedral mosque, the Jumna Musjid, is the most imposing religious edifice in the Peninsula. It is built of red stone and stands on an elevated terrace, approached by a lofty flight of steps. Upon passing any of the three gates we enter an immense paved quadrangle, with a marble reservoir in the middle, and surrounded by a cloistered colonnade.

The mosque itself, on the western side of the enclosure, is surmounted by three bulbous domes of white marble, flanked by two high minarets constructed of alternate vertical stripes of marble and red sandstone. "The whole," says Fergusson, "forms a group intelligible at the first glance, and, as an architectural object, possesses a variety of outline and play of light and shade which few buildings can equal."

Bent upon learning something of another Indian

THE JUMNA MOSQUE, DELHI.

faith, we followed our guide through a net-work of unsavory alleys to the Jain Temple. This shrine, although not large, is richly decorated with gold-work and intricate carvings in wood and in marble. The creed of the Jainas is a composition of the Buddhist and Brahmin, accepting and denying portions of both, but inclining to the former. This sect is believed to have taken its origin in the sixth or seventh century of our era, and a hundred years later it had numerous followers; but since then its influence has slowly declined.

Delhi is marked with many interesting reminiscences of the famed Mutiny. The insurrection first broke out at Meerut, only thirty miles distant, at which point all Europeans of both sexes were massacred. Thence the tide of fanaticism and slaughter surged along the road to Delhi, where the unsuspecting victims fell an easy prey. The faithful guards at the Magazine, under a brave lieutenant, rather than surrender their charge, applied the match and blew themselves to atoms. During the reeking heat of the summer monsoon the avenging army came; hundreds of outraged English to oppose thousands of mutineers.

Early in the fall the heroic band was reinforced, and then, seven thousand strong, including loyal natives, they assaulted the walled city, desperately held by a force outnumbering their own tenfold. After five days of incessant battering from fifty guns, two breaches were effected; but it was also deemed necessary to mine one of the gates. A perilous task, indeed, in the face of a murderous fire. But a fearless little party stood ready for the work. At daylight they sprang from their lairs with bags of powder, darted across the moat, and laid them by the Cashmere Gate. Some fell by the way, but enough succeeded in the daring attempt.

Then the fuse had to be lighted. One by one they dropped, but the torch advanced. At last the fuse burned, and in a moment the massive gate lay shattered by the explosion. Then the bugle sounded, and with a cheer the storming party dashed into the city, winning their way to the palace by the bayonet. A victory was won, but with the gallant young commanding general numbered among the slain. The authority of the government was restored, the traitorous old king dethroned and exiled, and his brutal sons were shot before their followers in the Chadney Chook. So fitly ended the Mogul dynasty.

Delhi has now less than two hundred thousand

THE KOOTUB MINAR, OLD DELHI.

population, but it once had almost two millions. The remains of the cities which preceded the present one are strewn in profusion over the neighboring plain, covering a distance of nearly sixty square miles. Temples and mosques, tombs and palaces, walls and forts, are here crumbling and falling, unheeded and deserted.

In the midst of this decay is the magnificent Kootub Minar, the loftiest independent tower on the globe, excepting the Washington Monument. Although it has stood nearly seven hundred years, time has scarcely marred this noble achievement of Pathan architecture, unquestionably one of the wonders of the mediæval world. It far surpasses either the Campanile of Florence or the Giralda of Seville; while the tower of the Kremlin, probably the highest in Europe, is unworthy of comparison, because of its inferior construction.

We spent two days in exploring this vast area of ruins, and marvelled at the infinite waste which man has committed in the name of religion and through vain efforts to perpetuate his own memory. The moral of this sumptuous wreck, the fabrics of wealth wrung from the poor, is written in the eternal law of nations that the era of luxury is the herald of decline. A conquered race, dragging out a most abject existence, peoples this land of fabled riches; and the vacant thrones of the tyrant Moguls, symbols of a " Paradise lost," stand in the gorgeous halls of state waiting for Old Mortality to inscribe them with the words of Milton,—

> " They themselves ordained their fall."

As we rolled away from Delhi and crossed the Jumna bridge, the young crescent faintly illuminated the snowy domes of the immaculate Pearl Mosque. In the distance we could distinguish the tall memorial column on the commanding ridge from which British guns thundered their demand to the mutineers to yield the stolen city. When the train halted for a moment on the bridge we caught the martial notes of the English bugler within the embattled citadel of the splendor-loving Shah Jehan. The exquisite marble balcony, in which the Great Moguls sat to review their legions, was vacant, and the parade plain beneath as silent and peaceful as the shallow, winding Jumna.

> " The moon of Mahomet
> Arose, and it shall set;
> While blazoned as on heaven's immortal noon
> The cross leads generations on."

At the Ghazeeabad junction, a short run from Delhi, we joined the main line, which extends from

RUINS OF OLD DELHI.

Calcutta almost to Peshawur,—a sweep of fifteen hundred miles. Heading northward, with Lahore as our destination, soon after midnight I heard the station hands announce Meerut, where the outbreak of the Mutiny occurred (Sunday, May 10, 1857), under circumstances not unlike those of the Sicilian Vespers, exclusive of the question of justice.

Early the next morning we had our first glimpse of the Himalayas from Umballa, which is the point of departure for Simla, the summer capital of India. But we entertained no thought of breaking our journey here, as we had in anticipation a trip to Darjeeling, due north of Calcutta, where the sublimest of the "hill" scenery is in view, including the highest mountain of the world.

Towards noon we crossed the Sutlej by a fine bridge and entered the Punjaub, the Kingdom of the Five Waters, so called, in Persian, from its position among the affluents which unite as the Indus. This extensive territory, the most northerly province of British India, stretches to the frontiers of Cashmere and Afghanistan, and shelters twenty-three millions of people. It was annexed to the East India Company's dominions in 1849, as a result of the unprovoked aggression of the warlike Sikhs.

Among the spoils was the Koh-i-noor diamond, which was presented to Queen Victoria, to be her personal property. The father of the fallen Maharajah, Runjeet Sing, robbed the Afghans of the famous gem, and they in their turn had stolen it from the diadem of the Great Moguls at the sack of Delhi.

Our train reached Umritsur during the afternoon, but having arranged to visit that place while returning southward, we proceeded to Lahore, arriving there just as "the glow of heaven" was descending upon the land.

The rascal that drove us from the railway to our quarter in the "civil station" dashed along at so reckless a pace that the venerable gharry threatened a dissolving view. We shouted to him, but it was not his purpose to hear until he had whipped the lean horses into the compound of a second-class hotel, where the proprietor offers a bounty of eight annas (twenty-two cents) for every traveller. After some determined persuasion, in the presence of the servants of the hostelry, he was induced to take us as originally ordered. We presented our introduction, for the house was neither a hotel nor a public bungalow, and received a cordial welcome. There we found that homelike comfort which had scarcely once greeted us since we left our pretty châtelet by the Loire.

"The house is built on Mohammedan graves," said our host; "you can easily find a skeleton by digging for a few minutes back of the house. They buried about here until within twenty years." Yet this is now the choicest section of Lahore. The residences are more of the English style, and the gardens finer than any we had seen in India. There was the aspect of living rather than of only staying. The opposite is usually the case in an Indian station. Civil and military officers mostly comprise the residents—men liable to be transferred elsewhere. Hence they do little to beautify their temporary abodes.

Others hope or believe their stay in India will be brief, even though it may have already reached years. Home is the watch-word of all, however improbable its attainment. Lord Macaulay, who was a member of the Supreme Council in 1833, declared that an humble lodging in London was better than a palace at Calcutta.

Thousands of Britons are unconsciously serving the Empress-Queen like the Mitimaes of the Incas, who forsook home and its ties to control and teach the people of conquered provinces. Not less than the Anglo-Indians, the need of a protecting arm against the subjugated natives insured the loyalty of the exiled Children of the Sun to the line of Manco Capac and the mother-country.

Some gratify their longing for England, where they experience the sensation of being strangers among their own people, and find the climate unsuited to Indianized constitutions. Accustomed, as they have probably been, to having an "establishment," with obsequious servants, which even a slender purse may command in India, they find themselves unnoticed in the London world of busy men, wealth, and titles.

"At last I began to long for my native country," relates Imlac, in Dr. Johnson's "Rasselas," "that I might repose, after my travels and fatigues, in the places where I had spent my earliest years, and gladden my old companions with the recital of my adventures. . . . I now (having arrived home) expected the caresses of my kinsman and the congratulations of my friends, . . . but I was soon convinced that my thoughts were vain. . . . Of my companions the greater part was in the grave; of the rest, some could with difficulty remember me, and some considered me as one corrupted by foreign manners."

Lahore, the present capital of the Punjaub, holds an important place in Mogul history, and the plain which surrounds it, like that of Delhi, is marked with the ruins of its departed greatness. It was the chosen residence of the Emperor Jehangeer, whose splendid mausoleum, richly decorated with mosaics, stands on the opposite bank of the river Ravee from the city. Before his accession to the throne this prince was called Selim, the name under which he appears in "Lalla Rookh," as the estranged lover of Noor Mahal, the "Light of the Harem." But history presents a different story of this couple from that woven by the poet's fancy.

Jehangeer, who was a drunkard and of cruel instincts, already had four wives when he fell in love with the beautiful Noor Mahal. She was the daughter of a Persian adventurer named Itmad-ood-Dowlah, who afterwards became Prime Minister of the Empire. The great Akbar, father of the Prince, interfered and despatched the girl to Bengal, where she married one Sher Ufgun.

When Akbar died, Jehangeer sent for the object of his affection. Her husband naturally objected to the transfer, so he was put to the sword to remove the difficulty. The lady was then brought to Agra, where the Emperor awaited her; but she indignantly refused his advances. This was the "something light as air" which Moore, with rosy imagination, has transformed into a mere lovers' tiff, upon the occasion of the Feast of Roses, in the Shalimar Gardens of Cashmere.

The lady's ambition, however, shortly allayed her scornful anger, and obscured the memory of her murdered husband. She wedded the sanguinary suitor, and was raised to the throne as the favorite Empress. At this time she was a woman of *middle age*. In addition to these realisms, the veil of romance in which Moore has enveloped her is further rent by the fact that she was a virago, and given to unscrupulous political intrigue.

On the other hand, it must be stated that husband and wife were very devotedly attached to each other. When the Emperor died he was profoundly mourned by Noor Mahal, who reared the costly tomb in which she was afterwards laid by his side.

The native quarter of Lahore resembles all others, except that it appears to be lower in the moral scale. In the Anarkalli Bazaar, which is the principal street, there is considerable animation, and a fair display of lacquered ware, silks, and shawls embroidered with gold and silver. Afghan weapons

LAHORE, CAPITAL OF THE PUNJAUB.

have been in demand by the collectors of curios since the recent war; but the supply is about exhausted. Good specimens of Sikh arms may yet be found, as a rule well finished and graceful in design.

The Sikhs are taller and more athletic in build than their puny brethren of Bengal and the South. Under the leadership of Runjeet Sing, the "Lion of the Punjaub," their soldierly qualities made them masters over the whole territory of the Five Waters, with Cashmere and the Derajat.

After the valiant Lion's death (1839), the result of his sensual excesses, their passion for invasion and plunder led the Sikhs to measure swords with British power. They fought with desperate courage, but the war ended in the loss of their independence. The boyish Maharajah, a lad of eleven years, took his seat for the last time on his father's throne, and, in the presence of his court, executed the deed which transferred his kingdom to the East India Company. By this act he secured an annuity of five lacs, or half a million, of rupees.

The young Prince was sent to be educated in England, where he accepted Christianity and continues to reside. A romantic story is told of his choice of a bride. While passing through Cairo, on a journey to India with the body of his mother, he saw a girl in the American Mission school who so impressed him that he proposed marriage. Upon his return they were united, and have since lived happily in their adopted home.

Lahore has a Mogul fort, not unlike the one at Delhi, but smaller and of inferior construction. Close to the gates of the fortress, within the walls, is the marble tomb of Runjeet Sing. Lying near him are his wives and concubines, some of whom are said to have burned themselves on his funeral pyre. The mosques and tombs about the city, as well as the palace in the citadel, are of secondary interest. But we find among the remains of its former splendor traces of those "mausoleums and shrines, magnificent and numberless, where Death seemed to share equal honors with Heaven."

One relic of that storied past yet exists in all its luxurious beauty, Shah Jehan's House of Joy, the Shalimar Gardens. We wandered through the orange groves and erotic retreats of this elysium, picturing in our imagination the days of history and of song, when the marble pavements were trodden by the houris of the zenana, and the five hundred fountains, strung in endless vista, terrace upon terrace, threw their sparkling jets into the sunshine to greet the august presence of the Great Mogul.

We drove out in shabby state to the cantonment, or military station, of Meean Meer, three miles from Lahore, where the sepoys received us with the martial salute due to our exalted rank! Here we saw a hundred elephants, many of them veterans that had drawn the heavy artillery through the Kyber Pass and up to the gates of Bala Hissar. Puissant and docile, the giant brutes now stood quietly feeding themselves with sugar-cane, occasionally using a long stalk to switch the flies from their flanks. When the sweet tiffin was finished, one by one they marched to a reservoir to drink and be washed. The keepers drenched them by means of buckets, and the elephants aided the operation by spurting the water first above and then beneath their bodies.

At the suggestion of an attendant we threw a silver mite (two annas) on the ground before one of the largest beasts. The piece fell unnoticed, but in obedience to the word of command he groped a moment and then dutifully handed it to his rider. After they had bathed, a dozen or more formed a line before us, and, at the order to "salaam," lifted their trunks and sounded a stentorian chorus, in honor of two sovereign electors of the Great Republic.

We now prepared to turn southward, though not without keen regret. In the streets of Lahore we had heard the Persian patois, singled out the long black locks and flowing beards of the pale Beloochees, and recognized the sturdy frames and ruddy faces of the Afghans.

We craved to know the countries beyond the snowy mountains,—the lovely Vale of Cashmere, and the rugged fields of Afghanistan, where England and Russia are fated to meet in battle array. But time and the season warned us to abandon such thoughts,—doubtless forever,—and so, with grateful adieus to our stranger friends, we sped away to Umritsur.

The Sikhs, who form a religious as well as a military community, have made Umritsur, "the Fount of Immortality," their holy city. About the end of the fifteenth century Nanuk, the founder of their faith, taught them to reject idolatry and worship one God alone. Caste was abolished and other features of the Hindu system were improved; but in the course of practice they have gradually receded from most of the reforms. Their creed to-day is practically an adaptation of Brahminism.

HOLY RITES OF THE SIKHS.

The Ka'aba of the Sikhs is dedicated to the god Vishnu, the second of the Hindu trinity. It stands upon a little island in the middle of the sacred tank from which the city derives its title. A marble causeway connects it with the shore. Groups of devotees are constantly bathing in the "crystal water" to wash away their sins, and large fish, called the rhoe, come to the surface to be fed.

The sanctuary itself is built of the purest marble, and its aureate roof, dome, and minarets glitter in the sun like the Tartar bulbs of the Kremlin. On account of this ornamentation it has been appropriately named the Golden Temple. Within, the walls are decorated with gilt and high colors, disappointing in comparison with the richness of the exterior.

Upon approaching the precincts of the temple, we were required to exchange our shoes for woollen slippers, the same as in Ottoman mosques. A guide attended us, and we entered all parts of the shrine without restriction.

Inside, three priests sat on rugs beside a large cushion, upon or before which the faithful placed their offerings of food, money, and flowers. When it was the last, the worshippers were given a few in return, with which they made three or four circuits of the interior, holding their hands in the attitude of supplication and mumbling prayers as they walked. Accompanying these curious rites a band of native musicians played without ceasing, and sang with the shrill twang of the East.

For three months previous to our visit, Umritsur had been suffering from the ravages of a malarial fever. During that period, thirty thousand, or one-fifth of the entire population, had succumbed, and the mortality was still three hundred a day.

In view of this alarming sanitary condition we timed our arrival for the morning, that we might see the Golden Temple and the shawl factories—the only attractions—and yet leave by the evening train for Agra. As we drove to the station, after dark, a dense fog hung over the city; so rank that we deemed it prudent to breathe through a handkerchief. The cause of the epidemic was evident enough.

We spent the greater part of our stay in the stricken city among the shawl merchants, and in the noxious mud shanties where their elaborate wares are produced. Umritsur has become one of the principal centres of the trade, drawing travellers and buyers from all parts of the world. The weavers are brought from Cashmere, and the wool from the slopes of the Himalayas. We were conducted through a number of miserable houses crowded with the patient toilers.

A primitive hand-loom is the only machinery used, but skill supplies the rest. The pattern is written on a paper, which guides the nimble fingers in manipulating the myriad of pendant wooden needles bearing the colored yarns. Flowers and figures are woven separately and sewed together to form the shawl. In India these Cashmere *chudders*, the precious fruit of the loom, are worn by men of wealth and nobility, while in the Occident they are the undisputed property of the ladies.

When we arrived at Agra the great Mohammedan festival of the Moharram was at its height. In the bazaars, the shops of the Muslims and of many of the Hindus were closed, and the streets thronged with people in gay holiday attire. Nautch girls, wives, and daughters, all decked with the showy trinkets of the East, filled the windows and balconies, waiting for the culminating pageant of the day. As the procession approached, the crowd surged towards its head, and the excitement became intense.

Near where we stood the line halted for a pair of athletes, armed with shield and stick, to display their prowess at fencing. Every hit was greeted with a popular shout, or taunts like those hurled at an unskilful bull-fighter in Spain. At other points begging posturers sat by the wayside, twisting their limbs into all manner of unnatural positions, while everywhere drums were beating, shrill reed instruments piping, and a myriad of tongues chattering in wild confusion.

This feast, which lasts ten days, is sacred to the memory of the grandson of the Prophet, who perished in the struggle for the succession to the caliphate of Islam. Gaudy shrines, made of tinsel and paper, designed like the tomb of the martyred Hosein, are carried in the parade, or symbolical funeral, to the cemetery, where they are buried like the dead, amid demonstrations of rage, triumph, and lamentation.

Agra is essentially a Mogul city, and nowhere are the wealth and splendor of that oppressive dynasty evinced to a greater degree than in its sumptuous monuments. Here Akbar located his capital and built the imposing citadel which overhangs the Jumna. Within its crenellated walls, a mile and a half in circuit, stand the architectural gems, some in a condition of ruin, which attest the magnificence of the imperial court.

After passing the massive gateway of the enclosure, itself a fortress, and crossing a garden, we come to the Hall of Public Audience. Next we enter the zenana, where the beauty of the East was once gathered, and then the luxurious baths, all lavishly adorned, which resemble the cool retreats and sprinkling fountains of the Alhambra. One of these chambers and its passages, called the Palace of Glass, are decorated with little mirrors, similar to the room at Ambher.

The Hall of Private Audience consists of two pavilions, smaller than the one at Delhi and more of the Hindu style, but almost as richly finished. Here we found the Black Throne of Akbar, upon which we coiled ourselves in Oriental fashion, without, however, feeling like a Great Mogul.

Then follow the elegant private apartments of the Emperor, and pavilions, kiosks, and balconies overlooking the river, seventy feet below, all of snowy marble, with exquisite fretted lattices of the same material and inlaid with mosaics of precious stones.

Near by is the immaculate Pearl Mosque, which is much larger than its queenly namesake at Delhi. Although purely Saracenic in style, this edifice depends for its exalted effect upon absolute simplicity of outline and graceful proportion, eschewing almost all ornament. The whole is of white marble, from the pavement of the court to the three crowning domes, "silvery bubbles which have rested a moment on its walls, and which the next breeze will sweep away."

Even while the Fort was in process of construction, Akbar was engaged in rearing a stupendous summer establishment about twenty miles from Agra.

The ruins of this city, for such it is, are within a walled park, seven miles in circumference, embracing the present villages of Futtehpur and Sikri. The plateau of a long, rocky hill, in the centre of the enclosure, was selected for the court, and upon this site arose a prodigal array of stately piles. Red sandstone is the prevailing material, but considerable marble was also used. Many of these structures are yet intact, while others exist in a state of partial decay.

According to the statements of early travellers, Akbar once intended this "most noble city" for his seat of government. Scarcely, however, was it completed before he quitted the place for sanitary reasons. Palaces and mosques, zenanas and baths, walls and towers, tombs and gateways, pavilions, courts, and halls, built with the money and the

AKBAR'S PALACE, AGRA.

labor of his subjects, were thus abandoned to neglect and decline.

This transitory paradise seems to have owed its creation to the advice of a fakir, or holy mendicant, named Shekh Selim,—whose marble tomb stands in the quadrangle of the mosque,—to commemorate the birth of the child that became the Emperor Jehangeer. Legend has interwoven its story with the history of this event, but in whatever light it may be viewed, we must conclude that Akbar either abetted a fraud or yielded to the baldest superstition.

But with all his faults, Akbar was the greatest prince that ever sat on the throne of the Moguls. Although constantly at war, he never lost a battle. During his reign the dominion of the empire was vastly extended, and wise reforms were successfully introduced. While a Mohammedan by birth and education, he was tolerant of all religions. At one time he inclined to a belief in Christ, when he married the alleged Christian lady, the Miriam of Whittier's exquisite poem, whose tomb is pointed out near his own superb mausoleum at Secundra, a short drive from Agra. He invited Hindus to accept civil and military offices, and chose two wives of that faith.

Akbar's efforts to establish religious equality finally led him to devise an eclectic creed, which sought to unite the followers of Christ, of Zoroaster, of Brahma, and of Mohammed. In this impossible task he naturally encountered failure, and the abnormal system died with its founder.

Every department of his court was sustained upon a scale of splendor before unknown in India. Under him and his successors, Agra blended the magnificence of the palaces of Nineveh and the temples of Babylon with the enchantments of the sylvan elysium of Cashmere.

Yet after the recital of all this wondrous grandeur the crowning glory of Agra and of India remains to be told. The incomparable Taj Mahal, that peerless marvel of love, of skill, of patience, of beauty, of treasure, and of power; the faultless, dazzling mausoleum which Shah Jehan raised to the memory of his beautiful, idolized consort, in accordance with a promise made beside her death-bed. As a last request she begged of him a memorial befitting a queen. In response he vowed to rear above her remains a sepulchre that the world should hold matchless.

More than two centuries have elapsed since this shrine of affection was completed. Attracted by its fame, in that period travellers from every clime have journeyed to Agra to behold the jewelled wonder. Man is critical, either from instinct or pedantry; but a single voice is yet to deny that Shah Jehan has redeemed the fullest measure of his pledge.

The Taj, which signifies a crown, is the work of the enforced labor of twenty thousand men for seventeen years. Scantily fed as they were, thousands died of want and disease, but this mattered little when the purpose of a Mogul was at stake. Like Peter the Great, when myriads perished in the swamps of the Neva to found St. Petersburg, Shah Jehan simply ordered the ranks to be replenished. Rajahs and nabobs were placed under tribute for a crore (ten millions) of rupees, more than half the entire expense, and the Emperor's private treasury furnished the balance.

In estimating the total expenditure (nearly ten million dollars), it should be remembered that the labor cost nothing except a trifle for its meagre support, and prices in the East cannot be compared with those of the West, even less so formerly than now. Marble for the superstructure and precious stones for the inlaying were gathered from every quarter, while architects and artisans were summoned from Europe.

I am conscious of the futility of entering upon a laborious description of a building with the expectation of affording much entertainment to a reader. Especially in the present instance, cold measurements and architectural terms jar with the poetic treatment which harmonizes with this ideal creation.* "Like piety or like heaven," observes

---

* For the pleasure of the few wishing the prosaic details of the Taj, I append the following extract from Fergusson's "History of Architecture":

"The enclosure, including garden and outer court, is a parallelogram of one thousand eight hundred and sixty feet by more than one thousand feet. The outer court, surrounded by arcades and adorned by four gateways, is an oblong, occupying in length the whole breadth of the enclosure, and is about four hundred and fifty feet deep. The principal gateway leads from this court to the garden, where the tomb is seen framed in an avenue of dark cypress-trees. The plinth of white marble is eighteen feet high, and is an exact square of three hundred and thirteen feet each way.

"At the four corners stand four columns, or towers, each one hundred and thirty-three feet high, and crowned with a little pavilion. The mausoleum itself occupies a space of one hundred and eighty-six feet square, in the centre of this larger square, and each of the four corners is cut off, to the extent of thirty-three feet nine inches, opposite each of the towers. The central dome is fifty-eight feet in diameter by eighty feet in height. The total height, from the ground to the top of the gilded spire which crowns the central dome, is two hundred and ninety-six feet."

Dr. Butler, in his "Land of the Veda," "it may be said of the Taj that no man knoweth it save him that receiveth it." Learning from the experience of others how completely it baffles the efforts of the pen to convey a fair conception of its beauty, I will attempt nothing beyond a mere outline.

Entering a magnificent gateway, we find ourselves in a garden which rivals the charms of Shalimar. Before us stretches a lengthy avenue of the trembling cypress, along the middle of which a row of fountains toss their slender jets high into the stilly air,—a superb vista, a third of a mile long. At the extreme end, partially obscured by the abundant foliage, rises the Taj, so white and dazzling that it seems to be the source of the sunlight which crowns it like an aureole.

Approaching it, we mount a broad terrace of red sandstone, upon which are two mosques of the same material, one on each side. From this base we ascend to a smaller platform of polished marble, whereon four towering minarets, snowy and graceful, dart upward from the corners. In the centre of this fitting pedestal stands the Taj, radiant and of spotless white.

The edifice is square, but as the corners are truncated it might also be called octagonal. Surmounting it is a symmetrical, bulbous dome, flanked by four lesser bulbs raised on delicate pavilions. A lofty arched entrance, and twin pairs of smaller arches, pierce each of the four identical façades, adding an air of lightness and plasticity to faultless proportions.

The walls of the exterior, not less than within, are lavishly embellished with inlaid vines and flowing texts from the Muslim scriptures. Indeed, it is credibly stated that the entire Koran is thus placed upon the mausoleum. Everywhere the finish is like that of a jewel-case, in supreme forgetfulness of toil or treasure.

We enter the rotunda, and stand thrilled by a beauty and a solemnity which pass all expression. Lost in admiration we unconsciously speak, and instantly the guardian Echo catches up the note and carries it round and round the lofty vault, calling it back softer and softer, as if not to wake the dead, until it fades into profound silence. Windows of marble lace temper the light within, harmonizing it with the religious sentiment which pervades the tomb.

Directly beneath the dome is the cenotaph of the Empress, covered with mosaics of flowers and foliage, wrought in turquoise and jasper, carnelian and sard,

THE TAJ MAHAL, FROM THE TERRACE.

chalcedony and agate, lapis lazuli and jade, bloodstone, onyx, and heliotrope. Beside it is that of the Emperor, similarly adorned. Surrounding them is a screen of marble filigree, elaborate and delicate beyond all conception.

In a vault below the central hall is the inlaid sarcophagus which contains the ashes of the lady of the Taj,—Moontaz-i-Mahal, the Exalted One of the Harem. There, also, close to the bride of his youth, rests the faithful Shah Jehan. Deathless love joined for evermore.

We came by moonlight to this sanctuary, when all was silent save the rippling of the Jumna, which flows by its side; and, walking round the shimmering pile, confessed that "the rare genius of the calm building finds its way unchallenged to the heart."

i

CHAPTER VI.

SCENES OF THE MUTINY.

> Man's inhumanity to man
> Makes countless thousands mourn.
> BURNS.

IT may be noticed that I have rarely adverted to the landscape of India. This has not been the result of neglect nor of a failure to observe. In a word, from the Ghauts, or coast range, with slight exceptions, it is an endless plain, relieved only by an occasional pretty railway station framed in flowers and the picturesque towns and villages. The route from Agra to Cawnpore is equally monotonous, and so it continues to Calcutta.

It was nearly three in the morning when we alighted at Cawnpore, chilly and sleepy, amidst a gathering of shivering, timorous natives. What a contrast, I thought, to the horrible scenes enacted here early in the summer of 1857. We were received by the proprietor of the cosey little hotel, a veteran of Havelock's heroic column. Late as it was, he provided tea and toast before we retired, and promised to conduct us over the various historic sites the next morning. After breakfast we started in his wagonette, and, moving from place to place, listened to his enthusiastic recital until almost four in the afternoon.

Previous to the Mutiny we hear nothing of Cawnpore, except its pleasant civil and military stations and commanding position on the Ganges. Strangely enough, unlike other military centres of India, it was never strengthened by a fort; nor has one been constructed yet, regardless of the awful experience of its need.

The outbreak of the Mutiny found the city wholly unprepared for resistance, much less to enforce the authority of the government. Although the garrison consisted of three regiments of infantry and one of cavalry, there were only two hundred European troops. The sepoys, or native soldiers trained in the service of the English, revolted in a body as soon as they received news of a similar movement at Meerut and Delhi.

When Lord Canning succeeded as Governor-General in 1856, there were already indications of popular discontent. The King of Oudh had just been deposed and his territory annexed to the British dominions, but not without engendering a bitter feeling of hostility. One of the first acts of the new Viceroy was to demand possession of the citadel of Delhi, at the same time informing the shadowy Mogul that his son and successor would not be permitted to assume the title of King.

While these disturbing elements were at work, a prophecy was artfully propagated among the superstitious people, that English rule was destined to end with the centenary of the battle of Plassy (June 23, 1757), from which it dates. Such causes as these were sufficient to excite disaffection in a race "accustomed for ages to conquests, annexations, changes of empires and dynasties, absorption of principalities, and violation of hereditary rights, real or adopted." Only a spark was needed to fire the mine of revolution, and with singular fatality it came like a flash of lightning.

To keep pace with the improvement in fire-arms, it had been decided to substitute the rifle for the musket. The change involved the use of a lubricated cartridge, and this apparently unimportant detail ignited the country like a firebrand.

Immediately the emissaries of revolt spread broadcast the rumor that the government, with intent to destroy the sacred institution of caste, had ordered the cartridges to be greased with lard and the fat of beeves. The one would defile the Muslims, the other the Hindus. In vain the authorities strove to allay the fanatical panic by denying the report. Infection, terror, passion, and indignation followed in its path.

Later it was discovered that a conspiracy had been planned for a simultaneous rebellion of the sepoys throughout Hindustan. The time was well chosen; and so confident were the British of their tenure that the crisis was upon them while they dreamed of security.

Regiment after regiment had been withdrawn for service in Persia and the Crimea, until only twenty thousand European troops remained in the entire empire. This skeleton army, scattered in detachments, over a vast territory, was called upon to confront a hundred and fifty thousand sepoys and millions of the infuriated populace.

The railway system of India, now complete, had lately been commenced, and was of no avail to concentrate the scanty forces. Every movement implied a long march in the most oppressive of the Indian seasons. Hundreds of brave men succumbed from sunstroke and heat apoplexy before they could reach the enemy. The fiendish atrocities committed upon their people roused the English soldiers to almost superhuman strength and impetuosity. Their thrilling achievements throughout the Mutiny must ever command the admiration alike of friend and foe.

The outbreak of the sepoys at Meerut and Delhi at once placed Cawnpore in peril. Sir Hugh Wheeler, who was in command, hastily constructed a rude intrenchment, two hundred yards square, around his barracks on the plain. Within this slender shelter he gathered the English and a few faithful natives, in all about nine hundred souls, comprising two hundred and fifty effective soldiers, and the remainder civilians, invalids, women, children, and servants. To defend this earthwork there were only ten guns of small calibre. The rest of the artillery, together with the bulk of the supplies, had been seized by the disaffected troops, now in open revolt.

Flushed with temporary success, the rebels started for Delhi, ostensibly to report for service to the Mogul, who was to be the sovereign of the new Mohammedan empire. After marching a short distance they were persuaded by Nana Sahib, the adopted heir of the nominal Mahratta chieftain, to return for the purpose of destroying the beleaguered Europeans.

Eager for the apparently easy prey, the sepoys at once commenced the attack. But the task proved more difficult than they had imagined. Batteries of heavy artillery from the captured arsenal were brought to bear, and showers of musketry fire poured into the intrenchment. Day after day passed, yet the little garrison refused to yield.

About this time more than a hundred refugees from Futtehgurh, forty miles distant, while attempting to escape down the Ganges, were intercepted near Cawnpore and cruelly murdered.

The besieged had but one well, and that was so exposed in the middle of the enclosure as to render it perilous to draw water. Heat, privation, and the shells of the enemy daily increased the roll of death, and every night a fatigue party ventured outside to cast the bodies into a neighboring well. Thus, in the vain expectation of reinforcements, their heroic defence was prolonged for three weeks; exhausted by sickness and want, with little ammunition or medical stores, they were bombarded, sapped, and stormed.

Seeing no hope of succor at the end of that time, Sir Hugh agreed to a proposition from the Nana to surrender; but not without fears of treachery. Having professed friendship for the

English up to the moment of the outbreak, the rebel leader might again prove faithless. However, the situation was too desperate to be governed by doubts.

By the terms of the capitulation, all within the intrenchment were to be insured a safe passage to Allahabad, in covered boats provided for the purpose. Two days later the survivors of the siege left the intrenchment, escorted by the sepoys, and marched down to the river, some on foot and others in vehicles or mounted upon elephants. While they were yet embarking, and many of the boats lay in the stream near the landing, an agent of the inhuman Nana gave the signal for one of the most perfidious acts that history records.

A bugle sounded, and instantly concealed batteries opened upon the fugitives with grape-shot, followed by volleys of musketry from the crowded shores. The thatch of the boats was ignited, burning to death the sick and the wounded, and forcing the strong into the water. Bullets rained upon them from the banks, and troopers dashed into the river to sabre all that attempted to land.

Of all the men only four escaped, drifting in one of the boats, although the relentless enemy pursued them for miles. Those of the women and

SCENE OF THE MASSACRE, CAWNPORE.

MASSACRE OF THE WOMEN.

children yet alive—many wounded, scorched, and bleeding—were driven back to the city and imprisoned in greater misery for three more terrible weeks. Although the ladies were subjected to every indignity, strange to relate not one suffered dishonor.

The satanic Nana, more anxious to establish a kingdom for himself than to restore the Mogul power, ascended the throne as Peishwa of the Mahrattas. Elated with his triumph, he despatched a body of four thousand men to reduce Allahabad. Advancing from that city, the avenging Havelock, with his little column, only twelve hundred strong, encountered the rebels at Futtepore, and sent them flying back to Cawnpore. Three days later the impetuous victors again routed the sepoys, warning the Nana of his swift downfall.

Enraged by his defeat, before quitting the city the incarnate fiend resolved to wreak his vengeance on the two hundred captive women and children, rather than allow them to be rescued by Havelock's approaching heroes. The horrors of the frightful massacre which followed stagger the pen and excite in the most merciful thoughts of revenge.

Says the narrative of a survivor, who visited the spot on the succeeding day:

"The native spies were first put to the sword; then the cooks and sweeper women, who attended upon the prisoners, after whom the poor females were ordered to come out, but neither threats nor persuasion could induce them to do so. They laid hold of each other by dozens, and clung so close that it was impossible to separate or drag them out of the building. The sepoys, therefore, brought their muskets and fired a few shots upon them from the doors and windows. Then the executioners rushed in with swords and commenced hacking down the helpless, unoffending creatures.

"The fearful deed was done most deliberately, in the midst of the dreadful shrieks and cries of the victims. There were about two hundred souls, including children, and from a little before sunset till dark the fiends were occupied in completing the dreadful deed. The doors of the building were then locked for the night, and the murderers went to their homes.

"The following morning it was found, on opening the doors, that some six or eight females, with a few of the children, had managed to escape death. A fresh order was sent to murder these also, but some of the survivors, who had not been severely wounded, unable to bear the idea of being cut down, rushed out into the compound, and, seeing a well there, threw themselves into it without hesitation, thus putting a period to lives it was impossible for them to save.

"The bodies of those murdered on the preceding evening—some still breathing—were then ordered to be thrown into the same well, and *jullads* (hangmen and dog-killers) were employed to drag them away. The children who survived the previous evening's massacre kept running here and there to save themselves, the ruffians allowing them to do so for some time, till they were cut down, one after another."

The next morning, after a final battle in which the Nana was crushed, Havelock and his invincible command entered the city. Guided by a few trembling natives the officers galloped to the gory prison, still hopeful of saving life.

Too late! Not a woman or child lived. "One of the rooms was a pool of blood two inches deep, and the well at the back of the house was filled to within six feet of the brim with the dead bodies of the murdered women and children."

Such was the ghastly spectacle which greeted the brave men who had overcome all obstacles to carry deliverance to their suffering people. But it inspired them with that terrific resolution which was soon to destroy the human tigers and avenge the atrocious deed.

The sepoys fled as the English approached, but some quickly paid the penalty of their nameless crimes. "Rebel sepoys and others were daily captured and strung up to the tree in the enclosure where the ladies and children were massacred. Many high-caste Brahmins were first compelled to collect the bloody clothes of the victims and wash up the blood from the floor, and after undergoing this degradation, which they believe dooms their souls to perdition, sweepers of a peculiar class called *domes* (the mere touch of whose hand to a Brahmin is pollution, and death from whom is to be attended by awful consequences) received orders to hang the infatuated wretches." The officer who gave the signal to fire upon the boats was taken to the identical spot and hanged. So proceeded the condign work of retribution.

The fate of Nana Sahib after the Mutiny is unknown. When the British entered Cawnpore he fled northward, probably to the jungles of Nepaul, where he is supposed to have perished. Continued efforts were made to apprehend the human tiger, but without result.

In the winter of 1874 a man was captured in Gwalior who claimed to be Nana Sahib, but he proved an impostor. His purpose was surmised to be an attempt to ascertain whether the genuine outlaw might expect the protection of the Mahratta people. If the theory was correct, the plan failed in every respect, as the Maharajah Scindia himself disposed of the personator.

Few traces of the Mutiny now exist at Cawnpore. Wheeler's intrenchment has been razed, but low stakes mark the line of the rampart. Adjoining this site is the handsome memorial church, of Romanesque style, called by the sadly appropriate name of All Souls'. Indented by shot and shell, the well yet stands from which the besieged drew water with such peril. The one into which the dead were thrown, night after night, has been filled and surmounted by a monument.

The fatal bungalow and its neighboring well have been consecrated by a garden of flowers and evergreens, nearly fifty acres in extent. Although the house of death has disappeared, a black marble slab indicates its position. The memorable well is crowned by the marble figure of an angel,—emblematical of martyrdom and victory,—and enclosed by a high octagonal screen, Gothic in design. All is fair to the eye, but the horrible associations of the spot ever haunt the mind. The pedestal of the statue bears this inscription:

"Sacred to the perpetual memory of the great company of Christian people, chiefly women and children, who, near this spot, were cruelly massacred by the followers of the rebel Nana Dhoondoo Punth, of Bithoor; and cast, the dying with the dead, into the well below, on the 15th day of July, 1857."

Close to the edge of the Ganges we stood upon the steps of the landing, called the Suttee Chowrah Ghaut, now partly in ruins, where, in former times, widows immolated themselves upon the funeral pyres of their husbands. Here the Nana and the sepoys perpetrated the treacherous massacre of the garrison. Since that awful tragedy it has borne the name of the Slaughter Ghaut. A small, deserted temple and an overhanging pepaul-tree, at the top of the flight, bear witness to the rain of bullets that greeted the betrayed people.

In several places on the walls of the temple, freshly written in an enviable hand, were the words, "May God destroy the English nation soon;" the work, most probably, of a young man, Hindu or Mohammedan, instructed at the expense of the Indian government. If pressed in public for his opinions, the same craven would doubtless loudly protest his fidelity to the Empress-Queen.

Despite the material benefits conferred upon India by English rule, I am convinced that the masses are neither appreciative nor loyal. Education has proved ineffective to emancipate the native mind and to uproot fanaticism. Every expedient has failed to establish the power of conscience or to exalt religion into a controlling force. Outward piety and compliance with ritualistic forms, which are apparently engrossing, here signify nothing, unless it be the potency of superstitious tradition. Even the pretence of religion is brazenly discarded when money is the issue. There are, of course, many individual exceptions, but only thousands among the degraded millions.

In brief, the spiritual condition of India could scarcely be more lamentable. While venturing to rehearse these unhappy truths, I am far from wishing to discourage missionary labors. On the contrary, the extremely remote prospect of regeneration depends mainly upon the evangelists for development. May they be inspired with renewed strength to prosecute their arduous task.

We journeyed to Lucknow, fifty miles from Cawnpore, by the slowest of midnight trains upon a branch railway. It was dawn when we drove through the silent streets to the cheerless hotel, thinking how narrowly the city had escaped a history identical with that of Cawnpore.

Lucknow is the capital of Oudh, and a populous Muslim centre. From a distance it presents an impressive *ensemble* of imposing buildings, crowned with swelling domes and arrowy minarets. But the grandeur is an illusion quickly dispelled by a nearer view.

The architecture of the court section is a tawdry mixture of the Oriental with debased Italian. Stucco, daubed with ochre, gilding, and whitewash, is chiefly the material. Such is the Kaiser Bagh (Emperor's Garden) Palace,—the late residence of the dethroned tyrant, now at Calcutta,—an immense quadrangle hinting an imitation of the Palais Royal of Paris. Everywhere above the door-ways and arches is the carved fish, the armorial device of the kings, denoting sovereignty.

Another huge pile of similar construction, called the Great Imambara, or Patriarch's Place, was formerly consecrated to the Moharram, the Muslim festival described in connection with Agra. Then, in the suburbs, there is a fantastic and almost grotesque suggestion of Versailles, known as the Mar-

ENTRANCE TO THE BAZAAR, LUCKNOW.

tinière. It was built by a soldier of fortune, General Claude Martine, a Frenchman, who became wealthy at the court of Oudh. In accordance with his endowment, it now serves as a school, and the founder's remains lie in the crypt beneath.

Although there are numerous tombs and mosques, Lucknow contains no eminently sacred shrine except the Residency. About that ruined pile is woven the story of one of the most remarkable struggles of history, the siege and relief of Lucknow.

Fortunately, the outbreak of the Mutiny found Sir Henry Lawrence Commissioner of Oudh. A veteran in Indian life, able and resolute, he early discerned the approaching danger and met it with vigorous measures. In consequence of the recent annexation of Oudh, an act of doubtful policy, the spirit of disloyalty was easily propagated by the deposed king and the landed aristocracy.

Against seven hundred British troops there were nine Indian regiments, in all seven thousand men, quartered about Lucknow. Although the bulk of the sepoys eventually revolted, the vigilance of Sir Henry delayed the crisis long enough to enable him to collect stores and prepare for the worst. After meeting with a serious reverse, on account of the treachery of his native gunners, the commander was compelled to destroy the only fort of the station. This enabled him to concentrate his little force to defend the Residency, already intrenched, where he had gathered the civilians and their families.

The undulating grounds of the Residency, some acres in area, form a slight eminence upon which are scattered the mansion of the former English political residents and the houses of officials,—all now in picturesque and sorrowful ruin.

Within this shelter, rudely adapted as a fortress, the devoted English withstood a desperate siege of nearly five months, bravely repelling every furious onslaught and heroically enduring the burning heat, privation, sickness, and death. At first they numbered twenty-two hundred souls, including the garrison of five hundred European soldiers, and half as many more faithful sepoys. The investing force is variously estimated from fifty thousand to a hundred thousand. As the prospect of reducing the place rose or fell, so the ferocious swarm increased or diminished.

Two days after the siege began, Sir Henry Lawrence was struck by a shell which burst in his room. Forty-eight hours later he died in the house of the surgeon, whither he had been carried. With no ordinary sensation the stranger now visits those hallowed spots, amid the verdure with which nature has draped the shattered buildings. "Here Sir Henry Lawrence was wounded," and "Here Sir Henry Lawrence died."

Benevolent and talented, he was beloved alike by the natives and his countrymen. The Residency is his monument, and within its grounds, in the little cemetery, we read upon a simple marble slab, "Here lies Henry Lawrence, who tried to do his duty. May God have mercy on his soul."

For three months after the death of their chivalrous leader, the beleaguered people sustained the siege unchanged. Meanwhile, a friendly native, who had succeeded in passing the lines by night, brought the glad news that Havelock was coming. But the gallant victor of Cawnpore, dreading to hear of another massacre at Lucknow, had hurried from the former city, in the reeking heat of the monsoon, with only fourteen hundred men, all he could muster. After marching four days he met and defeated twelve thousand of the enemy, and shortly after cleared a walled village by storm. Beset by insuperable difficulties, with sunstroke, wounds, and cholera thinning his ranks, he saw the hopelessness of his undertaking.

Then came the intelligence that a body of four

thousand rebels threatened Cawnpore, where only a slender guard had been left. Accepting the inevitable, Havelock started to retrace his steps; but finding his column pursued, he turned again and routed a large force. Proceeding once more towards Cawnpore, he attacked the rebels who were menacing that city, and drove them in confusion from their encampment.

About a month later reinforcements arrived under Sir James Outram, who generously waived his superior rank and served as a volunteer, that the honor of saving Lucknow might not be taken from Havelock. Without delay the hero of ten victories again advanced to the relief of the imperilled Residency, this time with twenty-five hundred men.

Overcoming all obstacles, in a few days he reached the outskirts of Lucknow and captured the Alum Bagh, a palace surrounded by a wall. Leaving his impedimenta within this enclosure, he led his determined command into the city, fighting through streets of loopholed houses and carrying the Kaiser Bagh, after a terrible contest.

The battle raged from early morning until nightfall, when the troops penetrated to the Residency and were received by the garrison with frantic cheers. No words can picture the greetings and

GATE OF THE KAISER BAGH, LUCKNOW.

the joy of the deliverers and the rescued, upon that eventful evening. But nearly five hundred intrepid soldiers had fallen in the day's struggle; almost as many as the remnant of the besieged,—three hundred and fifty Europeans, and somewhat fewer natives.

The Residency had been succored, but the joint force was too small to raise the siege, much less to conduct the women and children to a distant point of safety. Thus situated, the defence was continued for nearly two months longer. At last came Sir Colin Campbell, afterwards created Lord Clyde, with five thousand men and thirty guns. The sepoys intrenched themselves against his army and disputed every position about the city.

On both sides the conflict was relentless, and no quarter was asked or given. A walled garden, called the Secunder Bagh, held by two thousand rebels, was breached and stormed by the Highlanders, who bayoneted every man. So furious was the resistance that Sir Colin was three days in cutting his way through the city.

The Residency was then finally relieved and speedily evacuated. Silently, at midnight, the women and children were escorted through the narrow streets and along the road to Cawnpore.

Three nights later the remainder of the garrison withdrew to the Alum Bagh, where General Outram maintained himself until Sir Colin gathered an ample force and recovered the city, four months subsequently.

Two days after the withdrawal from the Residency the knightly Havelock died of a disease contracted by toil, anxiety, and exposure. His noble life ended with his humane task. Happily, he lived long enough to hear that his services were recognized by his sovereign and her people.

I can recall no foreign soldier whose career inspires the same touching interest as that of Havelock. Lacking, as he did, the influence of birth and means to purchase military promotion, under the former British system, his eventual distinction was due solely to the natural ascendency of worth and ability. His exalted character is written in the words which were among his last: "For more than forty years I have so ruled my life that when death came, I might face it without fear."

We drove out to the Alum Bagh, where his remains were placed by his companions-in-arms. A clumsy obelisk marks the sacred spot, among the graves of others who fell at Lucknow. From the long inscription we readily extract the gem: "He

REMAINS OF THE PRESIDENCY, LUCKNOW.

showed how the profession of a Christian could be combined with the duties of a soldier."

We lingered about the graceless shaft, and plucked roses to press as souvenirs. The surroundings are not as attractive as might be expected, yet I was loath to depart. Truly, as our impulsive admiral said when voluntarily he assisted the British fleet in reducing the Chinese forts of the Peiho, "Blood is thicker than water." Equally with any of his countrymen I can declare in all sincerity, that I revere the memory of Henry Havelock.

CHAPTER VII.

HOLY PLACES OF THE HINDUS.

> It must be that He witnesses
> Somehow to all men that He is:
> That something of His saving grace
> Reaches the lowest of the race,
> Who, through strange creed and rite, may draw
> The hints of a diviner law.
> WHITTIER.

WE came by night directly from Lucknow to Allahabad, exchanging stories of war for those of religion. Allahabad, scarcely less so than Benares and Muttra, is a holy place of the Hindus,—the City of God, for such is the translation of its exalted name. But one fails to realize the expectation which such a title excites.

The real importance of the city is due to its position as the centre of the great railway system of India. Here the lines converge which extend to Calcutta, Bombay, and Lahore. Its strategic value is also great, as it commands the highways of navigation to and from the upper provinces.

To the believer, the halo of sanctity about Allahabad arises from its location at the union of the Jumna and the Ganges, the two sacred streams which bound the Doab, or Land of Two Rivers. The tongue of sandy ground at the junction is the hallowed spot, and here myriads of the devout resort, like pilgrims to Jordan, to purify the soul by bathing and prayer.

Annually this custom takes the form of a festival, lasting a month, when multitudes gather and the lowland at the confluence becomes a vast encampment. A peaceful Santa Fe, if we may so adapt the term which Ferdinand and Isabella used, on the plain of Granada, as a Christian guise for warlike conquest. Many come in ox-carts or with caravans of camels; but more perform the journey by railway or afoot, frequently from distant parts of the peninsula.

As the Hindu religion works on a cash basis, these occasions are embraced for the purpose of gain, as well as of worship. Owners of various portable shrines hold forth their efficacy; Brahmins read the Shasters in return for pious offerings; the makers of gods are present to vend their wares, and groups of Nautch girls find an abundant harvest. Skirting the temporary city, traders erect their streets of booths or bazaars, and traffic in merchandise and cattle, like their Russo-Tartar cousins at the annual fair of Nijni Novgorod.

Every twelfth year, when Jupiter enters a certain sign of the zodiac, occurs the Great Mela, as the pilgrimage is called, during which the concourse sometimes reaches millions. Upon arriving at Allahabad we were told that this extraordinary Mela would happen early in the following February (1882), the last having taken place in 1870. Preparations were already in progress to accommodate the expected throng, although the beginning of the feast was nearly two months in the future.

Conscious as we were of the importance of the approaching event, our position was one always so annoying to travellers. We were eager to witness so rare a spectacle, and knew well the advantages we should have under the guidance of our resident countrymen. Confronting these weighty claims was the urgent consideration of time. We could not afford the lengthy delay.

The fakirs, or holy mendicants, common throughout Hindu India, always attend the Melas in large numbers, begging or otherwise exacting food and money from the masses. This repulsive class, for some strange reason regarded with superstitious awe, is the greatest enigma of an enigmatical faith. While outwardly ascetics and devoted to a religious life, they are, in reality, given to every species of rascality and degradation.

Under the pretext of sanctity they almost dispense with clothing, often reducing even the rag about their loins to the merest strip. Their hair and beard grow wild, and become matted and filthy through want of combing. Instead of the ordinary turban of muslin, they twist about their heads a coil of greasy rope or else wear nothing. The face, breast, and limbs they smear with ashes from the funeral pyres, relieved with daubs of ochre, vermilion, or other color.

We noticed scores of fakirs with sensual countenances, and as many more with thief written on every feature. Some distort themselves physically, like the lazzaroni of Italy, or perhaps attenuate their bodies by fasting. All these disgusting artifices, difficult as it may be to conceive, serve to consecrate the human beasts in the eyes of ignorant idolaters. How such lives and practices can be associated with religion is a mystery which staggers the understanding.

These fakirs inflict a variety of tortures upon themselves during the Mela. One, for example, buried himself in the ground until only his nose and mouth were exposed, and so feigned to remain for several days without eating. But at night the knave walked out of his grave, and, without doubt, stole the material for a hearty meal. Others would roll themselves in the dust by the wayside, and howl piteously for alms.

While at Lahore we heard of one so confident of the power of his holiness, attained through bodily mortification, that he ventured to thrust his arm into the cage of an infuriated tiger. In an instant the limb was mangled. This sceptical tiger, a noble specimen, was in the Zoological Garden of that city, where we saw him in one of his most ferocious moods.

Adjoining the site consecrated to the Mela stands the Fort, a work of the modern pattern. It was originally constructed by Akbar, but the Mogul lineaments have nearly all disappeared. On the parade-ground within is one of the inscribed monolithic pillars, which the famous King Asoka erected (B.C. 240) in the propagation of Buddhism.

The leading point of interest in the stronghold is the remnant of a temple buried under the *débris* of ages. Upon entering this sanctuary, by a subterranean passage, we were shown hideous brass idols, with glaring eyes; the usual *lingas*, which are sacred to Siva; and a bifurcated stump, apparently yet alive.

The last, called the Tree of Knowledge, is believed by the Hindus to be coeval with the ancient shaft just mentioned. When the log ceases to display signs of vitality, the crafty Brahmins replace it with a fresh one, thus perpetuating the preposterous myth. Our attention was likewise directed to another object of veneration—the water which drips from the walls. This the credulous attribute to the proximity of a holy stream, called the Sarasvah, which is supposed to flow underground until it joins the Ganges and the Jumna, forming a trinity of rivers. In India, at least, one realizes the force of Goethe's line,—

Das Wunder ist des Glaubens liebstes Kind.

While at Allahabad, we visited some of the American missionaries, who are present in force and laboring earnestly on a stony field. They have a printing-press, schools, a Bible depository, neat churches, and a zenana mission.

Among this little army of workers is Miss Sara C. Seward, niece of the late William H. Seward, whose department is medicine. As a physician she is enabled to reach the harems of the wealthy, where access would be denied the ordinary teacher. We hold pleasant recollections of a neat bungalow, amid a pretty garden, in which we were the recipients of her hospitality.

We prolonged our stay at Allahabad beyond that of most travellers. The hotel was the best we found in India, the people and the surroundings were agreeable; so we took advantage of the opportunity to rest and write. Ahead of us, our next destination, lay the holy city of the Hindus, of paramount interest in our tour.

I had already achieved Rome and Jerusalem, and was anxious to add the third of the four principal sacred places of the world. The gates of the fourth are closed by fanaticism against all unbelievers, unless it be an isolated, daring spirit, like a Burton or a Burckhardt, in fluent command of the Arabic tongue. We passed its port on the Red Sea, doubtless as close to the guarded shrine as we shall ever reach. But after a short journey we are at Benares, enough of wonder for the present.

It was nearly four in the morning when our slow train dragged its weary length into the station, over the river from the city. We could find neither a gharry (carriage) nor a person to speak English.

FAVORITES OF THE ZENANA

Sleepy, shivering coolies stood ready to carry our baggage, but where? We repeated the name of the desired hotel, over and over again, without result. At last, one of the natives, a shade less stupid than the rest, indicated by signs that he would lead the way. Following him, with six of his fellows bearing the luggage, we walked down to the Ganges and crossed on a long bridge of boats.

There was no moon, but Castor and Pollux were poised overhead, and Orion sparkled amid the starry splendor of a tropical night. The throbbing city was hushed in sleep, and not a thing moved upon the rippling stream,—the sacred waters to which the Hindu comes for atonement, as the Christian pleads the blood of a Saviour.

Upon the other side of the Ganges we secured a conveyance and drove nearly three miles to our hotel, where we had further difficulty in rousing the drowsy servants. Thus we entered the holy city.

So ancient is Benares that its early history is lost in the mythology of the Vedas. But we can trace the record of its existence for at least twenty-five centuries. During that period it has steadily maintained its supremacy as the religious centre of India. "The Hindu," writes the Rev. Dr. Sherring, "ever beholds the city as a place of spotless holiness and heavenly beauty, where the spiritual eye may be delighted and the heart may be purified; and his imagination has been kept fervid, from generation to generation, by the continued presentation of this glowing picture. Believing all he has read and heard concerning this ideal seat of blessedness, he has been possessed with the same longing to visit it as the Mohammedan to visit Mecca, or the Christian enthusiast to visit Jerusalem."

Not alone to the Hindus is Benares consecrated ground. Here it was that Gautama, after he became Buddha, first expounded the creed which was destined to exceed all others in the number of its followers. For a time the new faith supplanted Hinduism in this, its very citadel; but was in turn driven forth, to found a greater empire in the farther East.

Like Christianity, flourishing as an exotic, Buddhism has ceased to sway its own Holy Land, which lies around Benares and northward to the borders of Nepaul. Yet such has been its triumph in the Eastern Peninsula, China, Japan, Central Asia, and elsewhere, that it dominates more than a third of the human race.

Benares, excepting the European quarters, is purely Oriental in aspect. Its narrow, winding streets, thronged with humanity and sacred bulls; its crowded houses, and airy palaces built by devout princes for their visits; its two thousand temples and mosques, besides innumerable shrines and niches for gods; its tempting bazaars, with rich displays of gold and silver embroidery, fabrics of gauze and cashmere, barbaric jewelry and precious stones, wooden toys and the famous chased brassware; its hosts of pilgrims, holy mendicants, Nautch girls, sacred monkeys, and patient beasts of burden; its fringe of palms, acacias, and venerated pepauls; its sunny skies by day and myriads of smoky household fires by night; and its pervading atmosphere of base religion, idolatry, and hopeless superstition, —all combine to form a striking picture of Indian life.

Accompanied by a tricky guide, we drove to the heart of the city, and thence, on foot, penetrated a labyrinth of alleys to the leading temples. Swarms of people, miserable, bony, and almost nude, shrunk away at our approach, lest by simply touching us they should defile their slavish caste.

In one place we met a procession of noisy fakirs, girt with rags and smeared with ashes and pigments, going to a feast which had been offered them by some wealthy enthusiast. Forgetful of their sanctity, our guide cleared the passage for us by thrusting them right and left, without meeting the least resistance.

Before we reached the first shrine, repulsive beggars gathered about us and became very annoying. Not uncommonly they are victims of elephantiasis or other forms of leprosy. They obtrude their loathsome sores upon travellers at every turn, thinking to force a gratuity as the price of relief from their presence.

A ten minutes' walk brought us to the famous Golden Temple, consecrated to the god Bisheshwar, another name for Siva, the third of the Hindu triad. The popular English title is derived from its gilded dome and tower. Within the quadrangle we first came upon the Well of Knowledge, in which Siva is supposed to reside. Why it should be so called is not explained. After watching the faithful cast in offerings of flowers, rice, and water from the Ganges, we approached to see its depth. One glance sufficed, as the stench was not to be endured a second time.

Beside the well is a large stone bull, which represents Siva as Mahadeva, the great god, when he unites " under his own personality the attributes and functions of all the principal gods."

QUADRANGLE OF THE GOLDEN TEMPLE, BENARES.

A few steps distant stands the temple itself, filthy and insignificant in size, yet the high Cathedral of Hinduism. We were delayed a moment at the entrance by the pressure of devotees and sacred bulls. Says Monier Williams, Sanskrit Professor of Oxford, whom I shall further quote, "The letting loose of a bull—properly stamped with the symbol of Siva—that it may be tended and reverenced by pious persons, is a highly meritorious act."

In the enclosure these consecrated brutes were eating the vilva-leaves placed as oblations about the many *lingas*, or egg-shaped stones, set upright in a base (*yoni*) having the outline of a Jew's-harp. "Temples to hold this symbol, which is of double form to express the blending of the male and female principles in creation, are probably the most numerous of any temples now to be seen in India." It typifies Siva as "the eternal reproductive power of nature, perpetually restoring and reproducing itself after dissolution."

In this rôle the versatile god has absorbed the province of Brahma, who is now directly worshipped in only one or two places. The homage due the latter has been transferred to the Brahmins, or priests, who sprung from his mouth and are "regarded as his peculiar offspring, and, as it were, his mouth-piece."

As "the repositories, both of the divine word and of the spirit of devotion of prayer," the Brahmins are alone permitted to read the sacred books. They are distinguished by a cord, composed of three threads of cotton, encircling the body from the left shoulder to the right hip; also by the purity of their features, preserved through the agency of the stringent law, in the Code of Menu, forbidding intermarriage with the three lower castes.

Siva, as we shall find, is also extensively propitiated as the "destroying and dissolving power of nature, the more active principle of destruction being assigned to his consort, Kali. In every one of his characters the consort of Siva is not only his counterpart, but generally represents an intensification of his attributes. As destructress she is Kali; as reproducer she is symbolized by the *yoni*, and as a malignant being delighting in blood she is Durga."

Hinduism admits of sects, like other religions. The principal of these are the followers respectively of Siva and Vishnu, the latter being the second of the trinity.

Although Siva commands the adoration of all,

"Vishnu is certainly the most popular deity. He is selected by far the greater number of individuals as their savior, protector, and friend." Vishnu is worshipped through his ten incarnations, which form a favorite piece of mythology for decorating the brassware.

But to return to the Golden Temple. In the small enclosure we were received by a Brahmin, who invited us into the building. There the people came in a continuous string, making offerings and drenching the *lingas* with water brought from the river. From the door of an inner sanctuary we saw the rounded metallic face and glaring eyes of the presiding idol. The Brahmins warned us not to cross the sill, as by so doing we should profane this disgusting object of divine honors.

I can now appreciate the fervent pleasure of Mohammed, as an iconoclast, when he led a victorious army into Mecca and destroyed the three hundred and sixty images of the Arabian pantheon. After completing their round of offerings, the worshippers turned to this Hindu deity and bowed their heads to the sloppy marble floor. This finished, they arose and tapped a large bell overhead, to call the attention of the idol to their gifts.

The god is supposed to extract the essence from

what he receives, while the dross—whether goods, money, or food—becomes the spoil of the private owners of the sanctuary and of the insatiate Brahmins.

Hence the immense profits of a popular shrine. As with a patent medicine, a fortune may be realized by skilfully advertising the virtues of an idol. Such is the extent of this trade in credulity that agents are sent throughout the peninsula to allure pilgrims, by intimating where religious efficacy may be had at the lowest rates.

A second temple, in the same vicinity, we found to be a cow-stable, harboring a score or more of those useful animals amid reeking filth. The cow is considered the most sacred of brute creation, as it "typifies the all-yielding earth." In another place we were shown the Well of Fate, around which lingers a characteristic superstition. A window in the enclosing wall admits the sun's rays exactly at noon, when a person must be able to see his shadow on the water below, or else death will ensue within six months.

All that I have related, however, is harmless in comparison with the obscenity depicted on the Nepaulese Temple. The building is of carved wood, with sculptures illustrating one of the books of the

Ramanaya, a sacred mythological epic of the Hindus. Worse pictures never served the worst of purposes, yet they are openly tolerated in a great city of British India.

Perhaps the Viceroy's government can explain why policy is thus carried to a point which libels the good Queen and her people. There can be no quarter for this diplomatic handling of brazen vice, even though it be shielded by a gauze of religion. Laws founded upon reason and decency should be enforced by an enlightened Christian nation equally throughout all its territories. Abiding results can be had on no other basis.

Benares is a city of strange sights, and one of the strangest is the Monkey Temple. Think of hundreds of those wicked little imps in a place of worship! Undisturbed, they chatter, quarrel, and wander everywhere. After the toilet and foraging, their chief occupation is war. So much so that the tiny ones cling to their mothers at the first alarm, to avoid the sharp frays. Outside the enclosure, they infest the neighboring streets and gardens, running along the walls and over the roofs of houses, pilfering at every chance.

We bought a liberal supply of sweetmeats and popcorn, at a little shop in the vicinity, and took a position under a large tamarind-tree, close to the temple. In a moment we were surrounded. Some of the monkeys, in their greed, snatched the sweets from our hands, while the stronger fought off the weaker. A few raps from our umbrellas settled the bullies, and then the feast proceeded quietly, but with extreme haste.

Yet these knavish cormorants are all sacred; to be venerated as an emanation from God and a manifestation of His presence, like certain stones, rivers, trees, animals, and idols. They are also revered because of their place in the Ramayana. When Rama went to recover the beautiful Sita, his stolen wife, from the demon king of Ceylon,— which is the burden of the epic,—an army of monkeys aided the forces of the god.

The Monkey Temple is dedicated to the goddess Durga, one of the forms of Siva's consort, who delights in gore. In order to propitiate this malignant deity the blood of kids or goats is offered before her shrine every morning. Here, for the first time, we witnessed the rites of a living sacrifice, and a repulsive exhibition it proved.

A Brahmin " did a pooja" (prayer) before the idol, and then marked the face of the doomed animal with red paint and hung a wreath of yellow

THE MONKEY TEMPLE, BENARES.

flowers around its neck. The head of the victim was next secured in a wooden vise, about two feet from the pavement, and a boy held up the hind legs until the fore feet were clear of the ground. While the neck was thus stretched out, the executioner severed it with a single stroke of a long, broad knife. The twitching head was placed on a post, or altar, and dogs licked up the blood from the writhing trunk. In another moment the Brahmin and the public butcher were both importuning us for money! An appropriate finish for so revolting a ceremony.

Every instinct of toleration is changed to one of antagonism before this frightful hydra of Hinduism. The more we see of its serpent folds, holding a hundred and ninety million souls in terror and degradation, the more we ponder how the noxious monster may be destroyed.

The great stay of Hinduism and chief protection against its downfall is caste. In fact, it forms the basis upon which the entire fabric is securely reared. Without this obstacle, the stronghold of the Brahmins could be mined by appealing to reason, and to the instinct which prompts man to improve his position. But under the existing system "the distinction of caste and the inherent superiority of one class over the three others, are thought to be as much a law of nature and a matter of divine appointment as the creation of separate classes of animals, with insurmountable differences of physical constitution."

The four cardinal castes are the Brahmins, or priests, who sprung from the mouth of Brahma; the Kshatriyas, or warriors, from his arms; the Vaisyas, or farmers and merchants, from his thighs; and the Sudras, or servants and laborers, from his feet. Below these are the Pariahs, or outcasts, whose vocations are the most servile.

These divisions, established by the earliest laws of the Hindu faith, rule supreme and unquestioned. The caste to which the father belongs is hereditary with the child, and by no effort, virtue, or ability can a higher one be obtained.

"The Brahmins," says Professor Williams, "constitute the great central body, around which all other classes and orders of beings revolve like satellites. Not only are they invested with divine dignity, but they are bound together by the most stringent rules; while the other three classes are made powerless for combined resistance by equally stringent regulations, one class being separated from the other by insurmountable barriers." Hence the unlimited power of the priests over the mindless, superstitious multitude.

A violation of caste subjects the offender to acts of penance or purification; and to become a convert to another faith implies complete and painful ostracism. With these facts in view, we can better understand why there are only three hundred native Christians in Benares, where the population reaches nearly a quarter of a million.

It may be asked, Are there any good men that seriously believe in this idolatrous faith? There are. Yonder, across the Ganges, lives the venerable Maharajah of Benares, a devout Hindu, whose earnestness and piety are reflected in a blameless life. To the poor, he is charitable; to the stranger, hospitable; and to all, kind. We were told by his heir that his devotions frequently occupy him far into the night. In the Council of the Governor-General, of which he is a member, no man is held in higher esteem. Yet he is a Hindu, of the strictest type. And there are doubtless many others like him; anomalies peculiar to the occult problem of religion.

Through the kind offices of a resident friend, the secretary of the good Maharajah wrote us that his master would be pleased to receive us at his palace the next morning. The note further stated that a carriage would be sent to our hotel and a boat to the river-side, that even in coming and going we should be his guests.

At the appointed hour we drove off in a showy equipage, attended by a driver and two footmen standing behind, all three in crimson livery. A light barge, manned by six oarsmen, bore us across the swift stream to the gate of the fortress-palace, which stands on the banks of the sacred river and commands a fine view of the holy city. Thence we were escorted by an official to the drawing-room, where the "young Maharajah" courteously welcomed us in English. His father, he said, had been engaged in prayer all night, and asked to be excused, as he was resting. Urged by him to remain, we talked an hour or more of men and books and countries. He remarked, with a tinge of regret, that they were unable to travel on account of the liability to violate their caste. I referred to Warren Hastings and his demands upon the rajahs of Benares. "Yes," replied the Prince, "our house has been weak since then."

During our stay his brother and an uncle entered, and although they could speak no English, we understood the compliment of their silent presence.

TOWER AT SARNATH, BUDDHIST HOLY LAND.

When we rose to leave, a servant approached with a tray, from which the Prince took a vial of attar and sprinkled our handkerchiefs. After that he placed a chain of silver tinsel over our shoulders, as a keepsake, and said adieu, taking us cordially by the hand.

As we crossed the court an officer followed us with a photograph of the Maharajah, which he presented, with the respects of his Highness. We then left, pleased with the hospitable customs thus extended to strangers. At the hotel we gave the scarlet retainers of the carriage a baksheesh commensurate with the depth of their parting salaams and the splendor of their raiment.

Another day we went out to Sarnath, to see all that remains of Buddhism in one of its holiest places. When Prince Siddartha attained Buddahood under the Bo-tree at Gaya, when enlightenment was full, he directed his steps to the stronghold of the Brahmins, to offer "Nirvana, sinless, stirless rest," to all that would enter the paths.

> "I now desire to turn the wheel of the excellent law.
> For this purpose I am going to that city of Benares
> To give Light to those enshrouded in darkness,
> And to open the gate of Immortality to men."

Here in the Deer Park, now called Sarnath, about

three miles north of the city, the great reformer first preached his new doctrines. In the third century before Christ the zealous king Asoka erected a memorial tower upon this spot, and later a Buddhist monastery and other buildings arose in the vicinity.

When the followers of Buddha were finally expelled from India, in the twelfth century, these structures were either destroyed or fell into decay. Nearly all are now so far reduced as to be of interest only to the archæologist. But one, the tower known as the Stupa, or Tope, yet stands in picturesque ruin.

The upper part of this relic is of brick and the lower of stone, forming a total height of about one hundred and thirty feet. Its ornamental feature is an encircling, triple band of sculpture, richly wrought with geometrical figures and scrolls of the lotus, both in the bud and the open flower. An aged, shrivelled Hindu, who pretended to conduct us about Sanarth, mournfully declared that he was a hundred and ten years old.

The culminating sight of Benares, and of Hinduism, is the panorama of the city from the Ganges, when the people are bathing. Early in the morning, soon after sunrise, the crowd is greatest. Making our arrangements the evening previous, we drove betimes to the river, where a native boat, provided with comfortable chairs, awaited our coming. Rowed by six men, we passed slowly up and down, over a stretch of about two miles, halting a few minutes here or landing there for unusual objects. A more striking picture of life and religion is scarcely to be found in the world.

Lofty palaces, in close array, overhang the steep bluff, while below, on every available spot, temples and shrines threaten to invade the stream; and high above all the slender minarets of Aurunzebe's mosque rise in bold defiance. The people submitted to the invading spires of the fanatical Mogul, but refused to accept his prophet's creed. They are of little use now, except to afford travellers a fine bird's-eye view of the city.

In several places foundations have been sapped by the river, until the buildings thereon are either tottering or have fallen in hopeless ruin. As they fell so they lie,—partly submerged; yet no effort is made to arrest the progress of destruction. At two or three points a colossal, grotesque figure, a god in plaster, is laid prone upon the shore, in ludicrous attitude, while other idols and *lingas*, smeared with red paint, are numerous.

Near where we embarked the gaudy state barge

of a pilgrim rajah was moored; and primitive boats moved past, or lay clustered at every turn. Large umbrellas, with plaited covers, are frequent, planted either singly or in groups, to shelter the devotees or those engaged along the river.

Ghauts, or flights of steps, lead down into the water at short intervals. From the foot of these, or a few paces out, the devout throngs perform their ablutions. This daily washing not only refreshes and cleanses the body; it calms the passions, purifies the soul of guilt, and does homage to the divine essence which pervades the river.

Men, women, and children bathe together or within sight of each other. Apparently, they think of nothing, for the time being, except the devotional act. We saw hundreds, perhaps thousands, thus engaged; many standing waist-deep, some preferring a seat by the edge, and others sunning themselves dry on the steps.

About midway along the river front we came to the Burning Ghaut, and landed for a closer view of the spectacle. Here were eight bodies, shrouded in cotton cloth; four in the process of cremation, two lying on the shore, partly immersed in the atoning waters, and two beside the piles being prepared to receive them.

The pyres were not regularly formed, like those at Bombay, but simply shapeless heaps of wood upon the sloping bank. We remained some time, changing our position with the breeze, to escape the intense heat and sickening odor. In the interval, a little knot of people came, chanting and bearing on a bamboo stretcher their burden of death.

Near where we stood a stone marked the spot consecrated by a suttee, before that inhuman custom was forbidden (1829) by the government. The Hindu esteems it a precious privilege here to have his "gross body" reduced to ashes, to offer his final sacrifice in fire. Many are brought to Benares in their last illness, that their absorption into Brahma and eternal rest in him may be assured by dying and having their funeral rites fulfilled on the brink of the sacred stream, in the holy city.

In these, as in all other ceremonies, the extrinsic piety of the Hindus is evident. Religion permeates their lives as blood does the human system. Nor is it less vital and unceasing in its influence. It controls every move, however trifling, and regulates even the smallest of household affairs.

Unfortunately, this devotion seems to penetrate no deeper than a compliance with the outward law.

It takes the negative form of propitiating the deities having power to thwart mundane plans. Everything is made secondary to the petty needs of the present. Greed of money overcomes the scruples of all classes; of none more than the Brahmins. The average priest will traffic in the sanctity of the holiest shrines, or be guilty of falsehood, or deception, for a single rupee. Honor and its demands upon manhood are utterly unknown ideas. But all this is the natural sequence of following such a monstrosity as a spiritual guide.

In brief, Hinduism is a false religion, from whatever stand-point it may be viewed. If we call it Brahminism, as some do, we see only the most evident pantheism. In its true aspect, the popular, accepted form, it becomes the grossest polytheism, a confused, impure mass of idolatry, offering no hope for the future except utter annihilation of the soul.

That I may not be charged with condemning this strange faith without presenting its defence, below is a paper which two Brahmins of the Temple of Kali, at Calcutta, asked leave to prepare for a place here. No alterations have been made in the text, except such as their limited knowledge of English rendered necessary.

THE BURNING GHAUT, ON THE GANGES, BENARES.

"Whatever we worship, we worship in spirit, and not the inanimate stones and idols. True it is, that to the external view we are idolaters, but we are not really idolaters. If we ask ourselves what idolatry is, our internal conscience will say that it is the worship of dull and senseless idols, and that a man cannot attain salvation by worshipping God without spirit and without holiness.

"But the Hindus are, truly speaking, not idolaters, for they worship the Most Holy in spirit and holiness. Strangers or outsiders may superficially think us to be idolaters; the reason of this is, they are quite unacquainted with the fundamental principles of our doctrines and the explanations of our images.

"Innumerable are the attributes of the Divine Being, the Almighty Father, the Lord of the World. There is nothing impossible with God. He can perform everything in His stage of the world. What we call miracles are not miracles to Him.

"Europeans and many other peoples of the earth think God is merely an invisible and incomprehensible being; but according to the opinions of our holy saints (*i.e.*, the Rishis of yore) God is not only invisible and incomprehensible; He is at the same time visible and comprehensible. Being almighty, He is both visible and invisible, both comprehensible and incomprehensible.

"Any one can make the objection that it is impossible for a being to be both visible and invisible, that the same being cannot be both comprehensible and incomprehensible; but nothing is impossible with God. Consequently, though He is the invisible spirit, having no shape, still, when we worship Him, He has the power of appearing before us, by taking any shape He likes, because He is 'the all-powerful being.'

"So we believe that though our Heavenly Father has no shape, still He has innumerable shapes for His worshippers. By taking the appearance of Brahma, He creates the world; by that of Vishnu, He preserves the world, and by that of Siva, He destroys the world. By taking the appearance of Kali, He destroys the wicked and gives salvation to holy and religious men.

"Thus our shapeless and invisible Father, the God of the Universe, has represented His three principal powers (creating, preserving, and destroying) in the three figures of Brahma, Vishnu, and Siva. Now everything happens in its proper time, whether creation, preservation, or destruction; everything shall be effected in its due season.

MANIFESTATION OF DIVINE POWER. 181

Thus the power of time, which is in no way inferior to the above three powers, is represented by the figure Kali.

"Various other powers are also represented by God in other different figures; such as the power of knowledge, which is manifested in the figure of Sarasvatty; the power of wealth, in the figure of Luksmi. Many are of the opinion that the Hindus worship many gods, but we do not; we worship God in His different powers in different figures.

"Whose power is it that so brightly shines every day before our eyes; that gives us heat and light, and thus preserves our life? It is the power of God, who manifests His superior heat and light through the figure of the sun. Whose power is it in the atmosphere, in which we live and breathe? It is the power of God, who manifests Himself in its vital and life-preserving influence.

"Whose power is it that brightens our room, keeps us warm, and prepares our food? It is the power of God, who manifests Himself in the glorious and consuming fire. Whose power is it in the waters and streams, that not only cleanses us externally, but by means of which our insubordinate passions are also checked? It is the power of

God, who manifests His glory in the figure of water, and thereby preserves mankind.

"So, in the great work of creation, we see only the power of the Almighty in different figures; and thus, though invisible, He is still visible. This universe being His body, we thus worship the different powers of God, and not different gods.

"As has been stated before, the Almighty is represented as time in the figure of Siva. For, as Siva is the destroying power, and the universe being subject to destruction through time, he is also time,—*i.e.*, eternity. If we examine the image of Siva we shall easily be convinced that the figure is a true representation of eternity.

"We see that Siva's body is covered with ashes, which means that everything shall be destroyed by time and ultimately reduced to ashes. Now, Siva being in himself eternity, and ashes the emblem of destruction, his body is ornamented with ashes. Thus we learn a great moral lesson, that everything in this world is frail and destined to come to ashes; that we vainly express our pride in worldly things, all of which must perish.

"Whenever we look at the three eyes of Siva, we remember that time has three eyes,—present, past, and future. Whenever we look at the snakes, the tiger-skin, and the human skull that Siva keeps about him, we are reminded that the snakes, which are so poisonous and unyielding, must be subdued in time; that the skull, which is preserved after the destruction of the human body, may be seen in eternity; that the tiger-skin, which alone remains after the death of a tiger, is like a refuse of that fierce animal in the body of time,—*i.e.*, Siva.

"Thus, in short, we learn from the image of Siva, that whatever is showy, proud, destructive, and fierce must ultimately be destroyed and absorbed in the body of time,—*i.e.*, Siva,—and thus it is proved that the image of Siva is a true picture of eternity.

"As Siva is in himself eternity, Kali, the wife of Siva, is the power of time,—*i.e.*, what Siva performs he does by his power as Kali. We see that the face of Kali is black and has three eyes. In the beginning there was darkness throughout the universe, and, therefore, the face of Kali is black (Kali being the power of eternity). The three eyes are the three divisions of time,—present, past, and future. Kali has four hands,—virtue, wealth, desire, and salvation.

"The hand with a sword is virtue, because it shows that by destroying the wicked and evil passions it maintains peace and prosperity, and consequently the virtue of the world. The hand with a human head is wealth, because the head is that of a peace-destroying demon; and if the demon is annihilated, peace is preserved, and our wealth (spiritual wealth,—*i.e.*, contentment) is saved. The hand containing something is desire, because it is the emblem of fulfilling the desires of all. The hand always raised is salvation, because it gives hope to mankind that they shall receive salvation after death.

"Kali is always standing over Siva, by which we learn that as the soul prospers over the body, so the power of eternity prospers over eternity. As the spiritual part prospers over the physical, so Kali prospers over Siva,—*i.e.*, eternity (Kali being the power of eternity). The grasp of Kali is very wide, by which we learn that everything shall be swallowed in time. These are the divine attributes of the Almighty, by which the mind of a true Hindu is always enlightened."

Now, let us contrast with the above a paper given me by Miss Hook, of the American Zenana Mission at Calcutta, who is an earnest worker in the cause of Christianity in India.

"We learn from the most ancient shasters of the

Hindus, that in the early ages they believed in one God, and did not bow down to idols, but were eminently a religious people. But before they came from Central Asia to occupy India, they had commenced deifying horses and natural objects. Not content with one God, they must have *thirty-three million!*

"Their ancient books contain some beautiful hymns and prayers to one Supreme Being; but as time advanced—not having any divine revelation to guide them—they began to lose sight of the Invisible Maker and to worship visible objects, such as the sun, moon, fire, wind, water. Alas, how low the human heart can sink when left to its own imaginations!

"The Hindu shasters give Brahma as the creator of the world. After this he makes Vishnu the preserver of all things, and then retires, or, as some say, goes to sleep on a lotus-leaf. He is worshipped little, but Vishnu, being considered as more interested in the affairs of the universe, is very universally worshipped.

"Siva, the third person of the trinity, is the destroyer, and is not less worshipped than Vishnu. His chief characteristics are severity and sensuality. He is depicted as sitting on a mountain, lost in meditation, wearing a necklace of human skulls; his hair is entwined with serpents that cling around his neck. His wife was at first called Durga. She dies because her father reproaches her husband, and is born again, and at different periods has many different names. One was Kali, signifying black, and her history is as follows:

"There was a very troublesome demon, and Siva being requested to destroy him, sent his wife to do it. If, in killing the demon, one drop of his blood should fall upon the ground, thousands of demons would spring up to torment the world. So they went up in the air, and there a terrible battle was fought. Kali was finally victorious, and cut off his head; but lest his blood should fall to the earth, she drank it.

"After thus getting a taste of blood, Kali became so furious that she went on killing everything that came in her way, until the gods, in alarm for the safety of the world, besought Siva to stop his wife in her proceedings. Siva repaired to the place; but his wife was not to be caught, so he resorted to stratagem.

"Knowing her fondness for a certain kind of liquor, he placed little cups of it all along the road he expected her to come, and then lay down to await her. His trick was quite successful. She came along drinking, and before she was aware of her husband's presence, she stepped on his body, and, in shame, put out her tongue. Hence she is represented as a hideous, black woman, with her tongue hanging out. The Hindus, when they are ashamed, put out their tongues in imitation of Kali. Her fighting so long very near the sun is the cause of her being blacker than Durga.

"The worship of Kali is lucrative to the priests. Her tongue is always of gold, and at stated periods a collection is made from the people to give her a new tongue, and the old one goes to the priests. All classes of Hindus make rich offerings to the shrine of Kali, and sacrifice goats to her. These pay their devotions to Kali in order to secure her assistance in carrying on their villanous designs. At the same time, they are not afraid to make depredations upon her person and shrine, and more than once she has been robbed of her precious ornaments. Notwithstanding she has power to destroy giants and demons, she cannot protect her shrine from spoliation.

"A great many stories are told of Kali; some rather conflicting, but all agree that she slaughtered many victims. She is also represented with their heads formed in a garland about her neck. On one occasion, after slaying two giants, it is said, with a human head in her hand she danced on the corpses of her victims until, in her ecstatic joy, she shook the earth to its foundations, and at the request of the gods, Siva repaired to the spot to persuade her to desist, or to dance more moderately.

"The Hindu shasters contain so much trash that one wonders that they could make any impression on any one with common sense. Stranger still, that a people should think of satisfying the cravings of their souls with such gods as objects of worship; but, poor things, they have never tasted anything better.

"As for the women, few of them know anything beyond the names of the gods to which they bow; but custom has its iron rule, and God alone can break it down."

To sum up, the chief feature of this patched, perverted, and complicated faith seems to be a gaudy ritual to appease angry deities. It has no eternity, but urges absorption into Brahm as the final end to be coveted. Its very gods commit incest and murder; yet the masses of India follow it implicitly as the way to their mythical Kylas.

CHAPTER VIII.

THE INDIAN CAPITAL.

It is a common law of nature, which no time will ever change, that superiors shall rule their inferiors.—DIONYSIUS OF HALICARNASSUS.

OUR allotted week in Benares was only too brief for what Bunyan would call "the rarities of that place." But the approach of Christmas reminded us that we were due in Calcutta. One sweep of five hundred miles, across the crowded Presidency of Bengal, would land us there—the living capital of India.

The journey consumed almost a day; but during all that time we saw no Bengal tigers, or Thugs, or other dangerous creatures popularly associated with the province. Thuggism, which means strangling and robbing the unwary in the name of religion, was finally suppressed in 1830. And the lordly tiger, like the bison of our prairies, has retired from the vicinity of the railway.

We did see, however, myriads of the puny Bengalees, in the many villages, towns, and cities along the line. In all they number about sixty millions, —not far from the entire population of North America. Their condition, as a rule, indicates a struggle for the meanest necessities, despite the fertility of the great plain, watered by the Ganges and its tributaries. The soil yields richly of rice, indigo, cotton, hemp, and opium.

While much of this penury is due to the nature of a tropical people, still the expensive character of the government is a prominent factor. With all its enormous revenues, gathered chiefly from the poor, the finances of the new Empire already show a deficit. This might be obviated if excessive allowances to nominal rajahs and rich salaries to officials were reduced to a scale commensurate with the means of the masses.

As a consequence of the present basis of remuneration, the scramble of Englishmen and educated natives, for lucrative posts, may be compared to the plague of office-seeking in America. British rule has done much for the political health of India, and doubtless this wasting sore will soon receive attention.

We alighted from the train at the terminus in Howrah, virtually a section of the capital, across

TYPES OF INDIAN SERVANTS.

the Hoogly. The river, one of the mouths of the Ganges, is spanned by a fine bridge, from which one sees miles of shipping in passing over to the hotel.

Instead of a "City of Palaces," our first impression of Calcutta was rather that of a "City of Bad Smells." Owing to the lowness of the ground and the consequent difficulty of drainage, many of the streets exhale an odor like that of decaying vegetable matter. The effect of this in summer, when aggravated by the intense, moist heat, is to render the place feverish and unhealthy. Then the viceregal court, attended by its legion of followers, migrates to the mountain air of Simla, twelve hundred miles into the interior.

This absence of the government for quite half the year, is said to be the cause of the want of good hotels in Calcutta. So brief a season is not remunerative. The best establishment, located on one of the principal streets, opposite the Government House, is inadequate for its winter patronage, shabby, primitive, and uncomfortable.

Every visitor is expected to employ two individual servants, a host of whom are always in waiting; one to attend in the room and the other at table. Without these slow parasites one would most likely retire to an unmade bed, or waste much time in the gloomy dining-hall. There are no bells, but "the boy" sleeps upon a mat outside your door, and often snores or coughs the night long. Soon after daylight the babel commences, within and without the house; and a little later your soft-footed Hindu steals in with the morning tea, uncalled and unannounced.

The instant a stranger issues from the contracted door-way to the street, he is beset by palkee-bearers, gharry-wallahs (drivers), and persistent venders of trifles, from a visiting-card or a cane to a hat or a parrot in a cage. Even when we started out in dress suits and white ties, these leeches ran after the carriage for a block or more, maybe to press the sale of a plumed bird!

Early one morning, while we were sitting in our room, the hotel began to tremble, as if a heavily-laden cart was passing along the narrow side street. Instead of diminishing after a few seconds, the quivering increased. We both instinctively rose from the chairs, and the boy then with us started from his seat on the floor. I went to the window to ascertain the cause of the movement, but saw nothing,—not even a vehicle of light burden. The mirror on the wall was now bowing to us, and the unused punka (fan) overhead swung two or three inches sidewise. An ominous rumbling accompanied the vibration, which continued about ninety seconds, and explained the phenomenon. We were experiencing our first earthquake.

During the day everybody talked of the shock, and the next morning's papers announced that it had been severely felt along the coast to Madras, alarming the people and here and there demolishing a house. The superstitious Hindus flocked to the temples to mollify the angry gods, or to cleanse the air of evil spirits, by making offerings and sacrifices, as they did when we were in Agra, upon the occasion of an eclipse of the moon.

The English quarter of the capital is not unworthy the aspiring title which Calcutta bears,—the City of Palaces. Its Fifth Avenue, called Chowringhee Road, is two miles in length, broad, and bordered with stone mansions, each set in its own compound, or garden.

Adjoining this aristocratic section, and reaching over to the Hoogly, is an immense common, parade, or pleasure ground, called the Maidan, six miles in circumference. This spread of turf is partly skirted with tropical trees, and ornamented with a lofty monument and several bronze statues, erected in honor of men prominent in Anglo-Indian history. Partially facing this park, on the side near the business district, stands the imposing, orange-hued residence of the Viceroy,—the Government House. Its design is not unlike that of the Capitol at Washington, reduced in size and elegance, and with the wings forming a crescent.

In the same vicinity we find the Eden Gardens, where a long line of equipages land their occupants just at nightfall, to promenade a half-hour and listen to the music. The spot is truly a beautiful one, close to the shipping and lighted by electricity. Continuing southward along the river, and the edge of the Maidan, is the Strand, the fashionable drive, upon which the pale beauty, wealth, and dignity of the capital gather late in the afternoon.

Lower down, we halted to visit the encampment of a regiment of Sikh cavalry, and farther on, to watch a game of equestrian polo. Beyond these, we entered the gate of Fort William, around which Lord Clive successfully struggled (1756-57) to found the British Empire in India.

The famous Black Hole, which was in what is now the business section, has disappeared. Within its walls, eighteen feet square, one hundred and

THE PRINCIPAL STREET OF CALCUTTA.

forty-six Europeans and Eurasians (half-breeds) were confined overnight, in the most oppressive season, by the savage Nawab, when he captured the settlement, on the 19th of June, 1756. Upon opening the door the next morning, a hundred and twenty-three were found dead of suffocation.

Another afternoon we drove over the bridge and through the animated streets of Howrah, to the superb Botanical Gardens. The enclosure contains an area of three hundred acres, and displays long avenues of various palms,—the sago, the cocoanut, the Mauritius, the areca, the talipot, and other species. Near the gate, a noble banyan-tree spreads its branches and progeny of roots to a circumference of nearly three hundred yards.

Across the river from the Botanical Gardens the deposed King of Oudh lives in royal state, sustaining about his palace the semblance of a court. His chief occupation is to collect tigers and serpents, which he exhibits to strangers upon certain days of each month.

One morning we went with the American Consul-General, and a small party, to the suburb known as Kalighat, to witness the offering of living sacrifices, at the shrine there dedicated to Kali, the sanguinary goddess. The rites proved the same as those described in connection with the Monkey Temple of Benares. As the time for the ceremony approached, a hundred or more people assembled, several leading or carrying kids. The appointed hour passed, yet all stood unconcerned and talking. After a further wait, we inquired the cause of the delay.

The Brahmin who acted as our guide then explained that the flesh of the animals, after they are killed, is taken away by the owners; but that the body of the first victim must be donated to the priests. Upon this occasion, it so happened that nobody had tendered the required present! Hence they were unable to proceed.

Recognizing this shallow statement as one of the usual mercenary shifts, we contributed an amount (three rupees) equal to the value of a young goat. This, our informant said, with a pleased expression, would overcome the difficulty.

The executioner now appeared, and the Hindus crowded around the wooden vise, in the area before the temple. But again there was a detention. This time, because the Brahmins officiating that day wanted *two* offerings for themselves! Such effrontery was not to be tolerated, and we left just as they actually commenced, more than ever marvelling at the Hindu religion and its venal exponents. Four priests, all of whom spoke English, followed us to the carriages, and there quarrelled among themselves about a division of the baksheesh. The incident will afford some conception of Brahminism as it exists in the capital of India.

From this degrading exhibition we turned into the thoroughfares of the Native Quarter, first passing through that appropriated by the invading children of Cathay. The Celestials are principally shoemakers, tailors, laundrymen, and wicker-workers. Beyond, in the China Bazaar, which has a mongrel aspect,—a mixture of the Oriental and the European,—we were solicited by dealers in English, Chinese, and Indian goods. Farther on, among the Hindus, the streets are narrower, and scores of Nautch girls sat on the balconies fronting the second floor of the houses.

In one of the most unlikely neighborhoods we came to the spacious gardens and palace of a Maharajah, upon whom the Consul-General was bringing us to call. The sentries by the gates saluted as we entered, and within the compound plumed cranes, as tall as ourselves, stalked about with fearless dignity. Upon alighting at the covered portal, a servant in bright livery ushered us into the drawing-room. There we were joined by the aged Maharajah and his four sons, all of whom had received an academic English education. The venerable father was ennobled by the Indian government on account of his wealth and beneficence.

Art is the pursuit of the entire family, and, with ample means at their command, they have loaded the palace with paintings, statuary, and objects of *virtu* from every land. Besides this large collection, they had been engaged for twelve years in laying mosaic floors of rare marbles, so elaborate as to rival the finest in Europe. In this labor of pleasure they work under the leadership of the eldest son, who prepares all the designs.

After viewing the different apartments, except those devoted to the zenanas, we were shown, in the gardens, a small menagerie and many tropical birds. At parting, the Maharajah presented each with a bouquet, and wished us a safe return to our country.

Calcutta has several notable institutions of learning, both for English and native studies. But, unfortunately, education has not proved as effective as could be desired, in the task of regenerating the spiritual life of the people. They readily embrace its temporal benefits, but few abandon the outer, if they do the inner, observances of their baneful

NATIVE BOATS AT KALIGHAT, CALCUTTA.

religion. The social penalties incurred are yet the great obstacle to a change of faith. If a Hindu renounces caste and accepts Christianity, he imperils the chance of a living among his people. Surely this moral, or rather immoral, despotism must sooner or later fall of its own pernicious weight; but the day of emancipation is apparently distant and uncertain.

There is still another avenue of hope for India, and one which I cannot but think is the most promising path. "Zenana teachers," writes Miss Hook, "are sowing a large proportion of the seed that will grow up and fill this land. We venture to prophesy that the women of India will yet take the initiative in the conversion of the nation."

If the mother can be raised from idolatry the child must follow. Better still, to reach the young girl before her mind has become torpid, from traditional custom and seclusion. As men are rigorously excluded from the harems of the East, only women can labor in this field. Such, then, is the work of the zenana missions. The American Home in Calcutta, over which Miss Hook so faithfully presides, assisted by other ladies, has twelve hundred children, mostly of heathen parents, under tuition.

On the afternoon preceding Christmas, we attended a festival of one of these zenana schools, when each little girl, in her holiday dress, came forward, as her name was called, and received a doll. A hymn concluded the exercises, and as the childish voices chanted the song of praise, I felt deeply the meaning of the occasion. Although conscious of the singing, my eyes and thoughts were upon Miss Hook. Pale and feverish from overwork, she sat quietly regarding the children, but with a play of light upon her features that was not to be mistaken. How great the value in life one frail creature can make herself! But a good woman is the handiwork of the Creator.

That evening we sat within the chancel of the church of Dr. Thorburn, the American pastor, and looked over a congregation that I would have supposed it impossible to gather. They were faces of the very color we had met in the temples of Benares and Kalighat. Indeed, after seeing them, I doubted for a time the accuracy of my low estimate of the masses of Hindustan.

Further reflection, however, recalled the unhappy fact that here are only hundreds out of millions in the depths. Dr. Thorburn has wrought earnestly, and to some purpose; at the same time demonstrating for the encouragement of others that toil is not in vain.

Society in Calcutta, the world of the viceregal court, is largely composed of civil and military officers, with a sprinkling of churchmen, rajahs, merchants, professors, and foreign consuls. Many of the natives have also attained positions of wealth and influence, entitling them to places on the Viceroy's invitation list. A continuous round of balls, receptions, and garden-parties marks the winter months. They are not unlike the gatherings in which fashionable Londoners so delight during their season. Yet with all these gayeties the Anglo-Indian pines for home, and looks forward to his return there as the happiest day of his life.

We regretted greatly to be forced to leave the city just before one of these events at the Government House, which would have given us an opportunity to see the notables of the Empire, under the best auspices. The Consul-General kindly pressed us to remain for the occasion, but the departure of the fortnightly steamer and our long journey ahead, impelled us to hasten on around the world.

CHAPTER IX.

IN THE HIMALAYAS.

> Fit throne for such a Power! Magnificent!
> How glorious art thou, Earth! And if thou be
> The shadow of some spirit lovelier still,
> Though evil stain its work, and it should be
> Like its creation, weak yet beautiful,
> I could fall down and worship that and thee.
> Even now my heart adoreth: Wonderful!
> SHELLEY.

HAVING explored Calcutta, we had now seen the chief cities and the great plain of Hindustan, stretching away to Bombay and Lahore. But as yet we could only boast of a distant glimpse of the mighty Himalayas. This we had from the railway at Umballa, the point of connection for Simla, the summer capital.

True, we might have visited that resort, which is located on the lower slope of the "hills." Or, there was nothing to prevent a departure from the line at Saharunpore, whence the beautiful valley of Dehrah Doon and the majestic views from Landour are within easy reach. These, however, we passed, in anticipation of a trip to Darjeeling. There we should behold the sublimest of the Himalayan scenery, and the loftiest peaks of the world.

Early in the afternoon of a warm, oppressive day we left Calcutta, from the Scaldah Station, and travelled northward by the new railway. In less than an hour we passed through Barrackpore, where the government arsenal is located, the scene of the affair of the greased cartridges, so memorable in the Mutiny. After running rather more than a hundred miles, over a level country dotted with bamboo villages, we came to the banks of the Ganges. Here, as there was no bridge, a steamboat carried us over the broad stream, breasting the strong current and continually sounding, to avoid the many shoals. During the forty minutes on board they gave us a modest dinner.

On the other side of the river we found a train with the usual sleeping-carriages, in one of which our *resais* (quilts) were soon spread. All night long we traversed a low, swampy plain, which abounds with feathered game. Early morning brought us to the terminus at Silliguri, about three hundred miles from Calcutta.

After breakfast we again started; now upon the

narrow-gauge steam tramway, then lately completed. Away the little engine sped across the deadly Serai, a malarious, marshy jungle in which no European can steadily reside. It forms a belt sixteen miles wide, directly at the foot of the hills. In this section tigers and leopards are plenty, and the untamed elephant is at home. That is, if report is true, as I never saw an assortment of wild animals strung out along the roads.

We now began to ascend the Himalayas. The tall undergrowth gave way to forest-trees and the tea plantations, for which the Darjeeling district and the neighboring province of Assam are noted. Higher up, the fields were adorned with flowers, yellow and purple, blue and lilac. Great clumps of bamboo lifted their feathery tops to a surprising height, and blooming creepers let down their rope-like tendrils fifty feet or more from the overhanging branches of the woody monarchs.

Boldly winding onward and upward, the miniature locomotive abated nothing of its hurried pace. Steaming and smoking, as if warmed by the undue exertion, it dashed into the hamlet of Teendaria, and halted for a rest.

In a few minutes our iron horse was again climbing the noiseless hills, now and then startling them

A HILL SANITARIUM.

with a defiant screech of the whistle. One moment, perhaps, the eye dwelt upon distant peaks or a gigantic ravine; while in the next, on rounding a slope, a panorama of surpassing grandeur opened like a vision. Below us lay the wooded summits, descending from one to another, and beyond them a boundless plain, ribboned with a silvery stream,

> "Murmuring adown from Himalay's broad feet,
> To bear its tribute unto Gunga's wave."

Now, for the first time during the season, our heavy overcoats were required. The moist heat of Calcutta had been gradually exchanged for the wintry mountain breezes. At times, the rails led us perilously near the edge of the precipice, but accidents are said to be rare. Even with such expedients, some of the curves are so acute that it was a surprise to see them turned by a locomotive. In one place, called the Loop, the line crossed itself on a bridge, within a length of about five hundred feet.

Familiar bullock-carts crept along the roadway beside the track, but they were no longer accompanied by puny Bengalees. We had penetrated to the region of a sturdier race, bearing the stamp of Mongolian origin upon their features. Many were leading black pigs that took fright at the train and attempted to bolt into the thicket, but were held back by cords attached to the hind legs. The struggle was very ludicrous, and invariably ended when, with his hams pulled from under him and his forefeet extended, the pig lay prone upon the ground, unable to move.

Amid these and other diversions, about noon we ran into the curious village of Kurseong, forty-six hundred feet above the sea, where we had tiffin. From this point, looking downward, the views were grand in the extreme; but the great chain above us was hidden by dense masses of clouds. The strange people at Kurseong occupied our brief stay there, but we studied the same types to better advantage at our destination.

Once more we took places in the small, open cars, and rolled away, followed by the merry shouts of the villagers. As we rose towards the snowy range, comfort demanded a rug for the knees and feet. Such a contrast with the sensations of twenty-four hours previous! The ascent now became steeper, and our speed much slower. We had taken a stronger engine at Kurseong, but it was tried to the utmost by the heavy grade and short curves.

Tree ferns and towering oaks, set in beds of wild flowers, here bordered the pathway. Occasionally, we came upon a gang of coolies engaged in clearing away one of the frequent landslips. Beyond Sonada—another of the euphonious hill names—we entered into cloudland; not a dreamy, mental territory, but a damp, chilly reality.

Once, the struggling locomotive stopped in a rocky pass, entirely out of breath; and while it waited to gather steam, we walked nearly a mile. The engineer declined our challenge to race the train, as well as a proposition to pull it as far as the next station. An Indian "peg" (cognac and soda), at the last bungalow, and the bracing air, made us feel equal to any feat.

Trackless gorges and noisy torrents succeeded each other at intervals, spanned by substantial arched bridges. Hardy peasants, of the hill tribes, passed in growing numbers; some driving buffaloes or goats, and others carrying burdens held upon their backs, by a strap reaching across the forehead. A few moments later we rattled into the village of Jhor, seven thousand four hundred feet above the sea. Snow was falling lightly, and piercing winds swept through the exposed car.

Our attention was at once attracted by a myriad

of rags, several on a pole, one below the other, flying from the shanty-tops. A closer inspection showed that they bore written characters. These were prayers, inscribed by the Lamas and hung out by the credulous, to paralyze evil spirits in the air. We were among the adherents of a corrupt Buddhism; tribes hailing from Thibet, the frontier of which is distant, as the bee flies, only about a hundred and fifty miles.

After leaving Jhor, the incline was slightly downward, for the three or four miles remaining to be accomplished. This fact encouraged our feeble engine to a reckless degree, considering the nature of that section of the line. At several bends, around which the train was sharply jerked, the step projecting along the side of the car fairly overhung the frightful brink. It may be a "triumph of engineering" to build a railway so close to the verge of death; but in the present instance, as an approach to a sanitarium, it has the aspect of a dismal jest.

We were now within range of the snowy "Roof of the World,"—facing august Kanchinjanga, next to the loftiest peak,—although the veil of clouds denied us the coveted view.

"There's Darjeeling!" exclaimed the tea-planter

at my side. Ahead lay a picturesque town of white houses, clinging to the slopes of a group of hills. What a swarm of uncouth humanity surrounded the few passengers upon alighting! Odd figures strove with each other, amid a war of words, for the privilege of carrying the baggage. Presently, we were climbing the ridge to the cosey hotel, preceded by two laughing damsels bearing our heavy portmanteaus.

It was the third time in India that young ladies had paid us such an attention, and my companion carefully noted this important item in his diary. The short winter's afternoon was fast waning when we sat down before a crackling fire, in our comfortable room, nearly thirty-five miles into the labyrinth of the Himalayas.

When we awoke on the morning after our arrival at Darjeeling, the snowy range was still hidden among the clouds. Had our stay been limited to a day or two, this would have caused a serious disappointment. But we had arranged to spend a week in the Himalayas, to benefit by the invigorating tonic of the mountain air. Even as it was, we were greatly concerned, knowing that it sometimes continues overcast or stormy for a fortnight. Indeed, the annual rainfall is no less than a hundred and fifteen inches. And now the leaden hue overhead reminded us of what might occur.

It was Sunday, a holiday on the tea plantations, which the pagan natives utilize for their weekly bazaar, or market. This was a favorable chance to see examples of the several mountain tribes, so we went down the hill from the hotel and into the town, on foot. Beyond the railway station, on the main road, thirty or forty shaggy ponies were ranged along the fence. About them stood knots of men, including three or four Europeans, bargaining, talking, or bent on the action of a little horse dashing to and fro, urged by a Thibetan rider.

Farther on, we turned into a passage lined with the usual Oriental shops, which led us to the open square where the bulk of the people were assembled. Grain, clothing, sweetmeats, household stores, and various trifling articles lay in rows, spread on mats, upon the ground. The venders, both male and female, sat beside their wares, occasionally a man in front, and near by his plump wife, suckling a child.

Above all others in the throng we notice first the Bhoteas, a herculean race hailing from Bhotan and the neighboring hills of Thibet. They have

PALACE AND TEMPLES OF A HIMALAYAN VILLAGE.

Mongolian features and retain the Chinese queue. Their dress is a long, coarse woollen robe, bound at the waist with a belt, in which they carry a formidable curved knife, a pair of chopsticks, and generally a pipe.

The women have large, ruddy faces, with high cheek-bones, and thick hair hanging in two plaits. A fillet, set with coral, turquoise, or glass beads, usually encircles the head, and a string of amber or of square pendants, mostly of silver, adorns the neck. Round ear-rings, so large and heavy as to deform the ear, and a girdle of brass or silver links, complete the array of bulky jewelry. A warm, padded skirt of wool, and a jacket of the same material, often in bright colors, form their outer garments. As a rule, both sexes are slovenly, rarely washing themselves, and seldom changing their clothing until wear and tear renders it necessary.

The Bhoteas, females as well as males, are the hill coolies and drudges. Apparently, they are never more content and docile than when bending forward, like Atlas, under a great burden, held upon the back by a grass band passing across the forehead. As a compliment to her husband, a wife daubs her nose and cheeks with tar, that she may no longer be the same dangerous attraction for other men that she proved for him.

The singular practice of polyandry exists among this people, as it does in Thibet. When the woman marries one of two or more brothers, she becomes equally the bride of all; and no distinction is made in fathering the children of such a union.

The religion of the Bhoteas is a species of Buddhism, similar to that of Thibet, and administered by crafty Lamas, subject to the Dalai Lama, or sovereign pontiff, at Lhassa. These greasy, begging priests wander about, leading an indolent life, and pretending to subsist upon charity. In reality, they derive a living by trading upon the superstition of the populace.

As one source of income the Lamas sell the *mani*, or praying-machine. This is an inscribed cylinder of sheet-copper, exceeding two inches in diameter and rather less in depth, which revolves upon a wire axis thrust into a wooden handle. Inside is a roll of paper, several feet in length, written from beginning to end, in debased Sanskrit, with a repetition of the mystic formula of Lord Buddha's faith:

"*Om! Mani padme hum.*"

By some Oriental scholars this is translated, "O! the jewel is in the lotus," and by others, "Glory to the Deity," or, "Salvation is in the lotus." The reference is to one of the leading divinities of Lamaism, the disposer of joy and happiness, in the belief that he was born from a lotus. These six syllables have attained such importance that the entire creed hangs upon their power.

> "I take my refuge in thy Order! Om!
> The dew is on the lotus! Rise, Great Sun!
> And lift my leaf and mix me with the wave.
> Om mani padme hum, the Sunrise comes!
> The Dewdrop slips into the shining Sea."

As the Bhotea counts the beads of his rosary, he repeatedly mutters this strange invocation, and turns the praying-machine,—easily kept in motion because of a small metal ball attached by a short chain to the periphery. A similar apparatus, on a large scale and worked by a winch, is found at the entrance to their shanty temples.

The services consist mainly in ringing bells, blowing trumpets, clashing cymbals, and beating gongs and drums. Along the roads and on the hill-sides they place offerings of rice; and sometimes their prayers, written on rags and tied to sticks, will form a continuous line for two or three hundred feet up a slope.

Besides the Bhoteas, in the Sunday bazaar, we see the diminutive but muscular Lepchas, the supposed aborigines, a lazy, nomadic tribe, fond of games and having many curious customs. The women have a weakness for trinkets, and the men for long hair, which their wives dutifully inspect (!) and dress for them, in the pigtail style. Conversely, a father demurely rocks the cradle while a mother labors in the vegetable-patches.

Then we find the Limbos, a family closely allied to the Lepchas, but braver and more distinctly Mongolian. Their faith is a mixture of Hinduism with the Buddhist creed; and they are said to buy their wives. Next, there is a proportion of Bengalees, with whom we are already familiar from our travels on their great plain.

Lastly, but most numerous of all, the active Nepaulese claim our attention. They are lighter in physique than the other classes, yet not less independent and useful. In their own narrow, mountain country, which bounds the Darjeeling district on the west, the Ghorkas, or dominant clan, are warlike and jealous of their freedom. Here, as well as there, they carry a heavy, wicked knife, known as a *kukery*. Nearly all the hands employed on the tea plantations are Nepaulese, the women being preferred to the men on account of having a lighter touch. Their belief inclines to Hinduism, but preserves certain Buddhist and early idolatrous rites.

On the third morning of our sojourn at Darjeeling we had a glimpse of the snowy summit of Kanchinjanga, but only for a few moments. Later in the day, when it promised to clear again, we walked along the upper road, past a line of pretty residences, to the Observatory. The position is a commanding one, but the clouds obstinately refused to leave the peaks. As a consolation, we could only look down into the wooded ravine of the Ranjit River, six thousand feet below. The stream is crossed by a primitive bridge, of rattan, bamboo, and the branches of trees.

The same afternoon, stimulated by the crisp air, we tramped around the hills, up one path and down another, in search of the Happy Valley Tea Gardens. Every step over the frosty ground seemed to add its quota of renewed life and strength, and to prepare us for the coming siege of equatorial heat.

Confused, instead of assisted, by the complicated directions given us in the town, we at length wandered into the compound of a bungalow, and received a polite welcome from three Jesuit fathers. Rather pleased than otherwise at our chance intrusion, they walked with us to a ledge overlooking a lower range of hills, and pointed out the Happy Valley, far below. When we finally reached the spot, the manager's wife, in his absence, invited us into their home for a cup of fragrant Pekoe, before taking us over the estate.

We were much entertained in the Happy Valley Gardens, watching a large force of hardy Nepaulese engaged in pruning, which they did with rapidity and skill. Young women with substantial ankles smiled among themselves at our curiosity to see their simple work, and mothers with babies tied to their backs were equally amused at being so closely observed. With few wants, happy, contented, and mindless, thus they toil, only too glad to earn a daily pittance of five annas, or about fourteen cents.

Our hostess duly took us through the low, white buildings, where, in the season, the precious leaf is submitted to a mechanical process. First, a quantity is subjected to heat in copper pans, or spread on trays to wither; next, rolled on a table or in a machine; then allowed to ferment to a certain degree, followed by a slight sunning; and lastly,

A TEA PLANTATION, DARJEELING.

exposed to a charcoal fire and there manipulated until it becomes dry, shrunken, and crisp. This product is passed through sieves of different sizes, by which the finer and better grades are separated from the others.

The treatment necessary to make green tea requires the unwilted leaf to be heated until the mass is glutinous, and finally, after the intervening stages, to be pressed into bags and beaten with flat sticks, which develops the greenish color. Thus we get our Hyson, Gunpowder, and Imperial. Teas are packed in cases lined with lead, and holding from eighty to a hundred pounds.

Tea is the chief product of the Darjeeling district, as well as of the adjoining province of Assam, and more or less is grown westward along the ridges of the Himalayas, for upwards of a thousand miles. The slopes of the hills, from two thousand to five thousand feet above the level of the sea, afford the best soil and location for its growth, with a choice in favor of the lesser height. At that elevation there is ample moisture, a vital requisite, and yet such as will freely pass away.

Many of the plantations are laid out in terraces, one about two feet above the other, and some in ordinary fields. The bushes are set in rows and pruned between November and February, leaving them about twenty inches high. Early in the spring the plant "flushes," or sends out new shoots six to eight inches long, which it repeats every two or three weeks, for a period of eight months. These tender leaves are carefully picked and sorted, those from the tip of the stem, or the youngest, making the finest tea. According to the selection, we have Pekoe, Souchong, or Congou, or various names in other countries. Green tea differs from the black only in the mode of preparation.

It was not yet light when we were awakened by a knock at the door, on our fourth morning at Darjeeling. The stars were shining, and the jackals still howling in dismal chorus, close to the house. Not a cloud could be seen, and the majesty of God was reflected from the mountain-tops. The advanced rays of coming dawn silvered the soaring peak of Kanchinjanga, while the snowy range, moment by moment, caught the glow upon its eternal mantle of white.

I had been writing until two or three hours past midnight, not daring to look at the watch, struggling to finish my lengthy journal to date. Upon giving it the last careful touches of revision, I went out on the porch in the vain hope of seeing the unusually bold jackals. At that time the heavens were still overcast; so I retired, weary and with a throbbing head, little expecting to be called so early. But now all desire for sleep was instantly banished by the prospect of realizing one of the greatest features of our tour,—to behold the pinnacle of the earth.

Kanchinjanga is in full view from Darjeeling, but not so with Everest. To see that monarch of mountains, as well as a lengthy sweep of the snowy range, one must ride six miles southeast to the summit of Mount Senchal. Jealous Nature was now pleased to expose this dazzling vision; but who could say for how long? There was no time to be lost. What would be our feelings if the misty veil should again be drawn before we could reach the distant eyrie! The path thither is such that a pony cannot traverse it in less than two hours.

In a few minutes we had disposed of eggs and tea, and were in the saddle. The two poor syces (running grooms), nearly nude and benumbed by the cold, barely kept up with our anxious, eager pace. Directly above the town, after a steep climb, we rode through the neat martial station of Jellapahar, where all yet slept, except the lonely sentries wrapped in great-coats. At one place we met a group of Hindus at their morning ablutions beside a trickling spring, and farther on a band of villagers came along bearing two stuffed tigers, probably in observance of some pagan rite.

As the sun rose and tinted the hills and valleys, the lofty peaks above shone resplendent in the purest white, against a background of spotless azure. So quickly had the clouds vanished that it was a wonder where they could be hiding, until we spied one resting like a river of cotton in the bed of a winding glen. Not far from our destination we passed the picturesque ruins of a town, aptly called the Chimneys, the remains of a deserted military sanitarium.

We left the ponies on an upper ridge of Senchal and mounted afoot to a cairn which marks the summit, an altitude of eight thousand six hundred feet. No words can picture the sublime panorama which there greeted our vision. It was a pleasure known only to those who wander over the world seeking the glories of Nature.

There was Everest, eighty miles off, rising like a sugar-cone above the intervening hills, twenty-nine thousand feet high. Then, unobstructed to the view, outspread, rugged Kanchinjanga, sixty miles

KANCHINJANGA, THE WORLD'S SECOND MOUNTAIN.

THE CREATOR'S SANCTUARY.

distant, which reaches twenty-eight thousand one hundred and fifty-six feet above the level of the sea. And, in addition to these presiding giants, the eye spanned a number of other peaks above twenty thousand feet in height, as well as more than a hundred miles of the "stainless ramps of huge Himala's wall." They stood

> "Ranged in white ranks against the blue—untrod,
> Infinite, wonderful—whose uplands vast,
> And lifted universe of crest and crag,
> Shoulder and shelf, green slope and icy horn,
> Riven ravine, and splintered precipice
> Led climbing thought higher and higher, until
> It seemed to stand in Heaven and speak with gods."

No! not the lifeless gods of the poet's Buddhist, nor yet those of a soulless pantheism, but rather that exalted worship, that true church, by which the quickened spirit, without the services of priest or ritual, is brought into the holiest communion with the Creator.

CHAPTER X.

THE MADRAS PRESIDENCY.

> Outside of Indus, inside Ganges, lies
> a wide-spread country famed enough of yore;
> Northward the peaks of caved Emódus rise,
> and southward Ocean doth confine the shore:
> She bears the yoke of various sovranties
> and various eke her creeds: While these adore
> vicious Mafóma, those to stock and stone
> bow down, and eke to brutes among them grown.
> CAMOENS.

MUCH to the surprise of all, the skies at Darjeeling were cloudless for three days after our expedition to Mount Senchal. Thus it was when we turned our eyes toward the snowy range for the last time, and sped away on the return journey to Calcutta. So clear was the atmosphere that we saw the peak of Kanchinjanga as far as Siliguri, twelve miles from the base of the Himalayas, and nearly a hundred from the mountain.

Our steamer for Madras, the "Ancona," of the Peninsular and Oriental line, was already in the

Hoogly, loading for the long homeward voyage to London. She was announced to sail at dawn, on the third day after our arrival, so we went aboard before midnight. The ship was moored to the quay at Garden Reach, a suburb below the city, whither we drove by way of the favorite Strand. There we dragged through a miserable night, tormented by the heat and hungry mosquitoes.

When we rose in the morning the steamer was cautiously descending the river, threading her way among the dangerous shoals and around the reaches, or bends. The low delta country is overrun with jungles, relieved only by an occasional mud village with its palm grove and fields of paddy. So slow was our progress that the tide ebbed before the sea was reached, compelling us to anchor for several hours.

This, too, in spite of the overpowering presence of our gorgeous pilot. Such another as he would not dare to exist on the globe. Sir Joseph Porter, K.C.B., or the commander of any other navy, could never hope to rival the golden splendor of his uniform, nor to inspire the trembling awe which resulted from his stentorian address and lofty, unapproachable mien. Besides this terrible array, everybody was further ground into the attitude of a pigmy by the fact that he never appeared without spotless white cotton gloves. I can yet see him pressing them into place by crowding his fingers between each other. It would doubtless have been death to interrupt the operation.

Not as a weakness, but rather as a source of strength, this personage frequently sacrificed himself by going to the bar for a cocktail. I do not refer to any of the bars over which he was struggling to guide us safely, but to a dangerous one within the ship.

During the enforced stoppage a rash passenger ventured to suggest a game of whist, which led to a frightful outbreak. "Whist, by ——!" thundered the magnificent, in a tone of withering scorn; "whist! Yesterday I took a steamer up the river; last night I went to the theatre; and to-day I am bringing this ship down; and yet you ask me to play whist, by ——!"

At last we were clear of the Hoogly, and steaming at full speed towards Madras. On the second day out we were almost within sight of Pooree, where the famous Temple of Juggernaut is located. Every March the image of the god is placed on an immense car, having sixteen wheels, and dragged through the streets. Myriads of pilgrims assemble upon these occasions, and formerly many immolated themselves beneath the wheels. Happily, this method of fanatical suicide is now forbidden by the English government.

The idol of Juggernaut owes its prominence to the tradition that it contains a bone of Krishna, the Indian Apollo, one of the ten avatars of Vishnu. This worship of a relic, unusual to the Hindu faith, is a remnant of Buddhism, which once prevailed throughout the province of Orissa.

Next day we passed Vizagapatam, whence comes the beautiful tortoise-shell and ivory-ware. Almost on a line directly westward from this port, and near Hyderabad, is Golconda, in the vicinity of which the great diamonds of the world were found. Farther south, close to the mouth of the Godavery, stands Coconada, which boasts a Hindu pagoda that competes in obscenity with the Nepaulese temple at Benares.

On the fifth afternoon we distinguished Madras along the low coast, and as the ship approached the city we exchanged greetings with the outward-bound steamer "Ceylon," then sailing round the world with a company of tourists.

Our trip from Calcutta had been a delightful one, —May weather, without a ripple; but a petty annoyance was in store for the finish. The rules of the port forbid ships to enter without a pilot and after sundown. As the distance narrowed it became a race against the sun, and we lost by the merest trifle,—not more than ten minutes. Less than three hundred yards from the mole the "Ancona" halted and sounded a deep appeal for a welcome, but in vain. A landsman might almost have taken the ship through the ample gateway ahead, yet for some unseen reason we could only anchor outside.

But it was a glorious picture, all aglow with the hue of burning gold which decked the west, over the town and beyond the hills. Rocked by the measured swell, and yielding to the revery so apt to follow a disappointment, we unconsciously stood

> "Looking upon the evening and the flood,
> Which lay between the city and the shore,
> Paved with the image of the sky."

Owing to a conflict of oblique seas, the coast about Madras is never free of surf. Even in the fairest weather the breakers roll in with tremendous force, and in stormy times it becomes dangerous and often impossible to land. A stranger wonders why so unfavorable and barren a site was

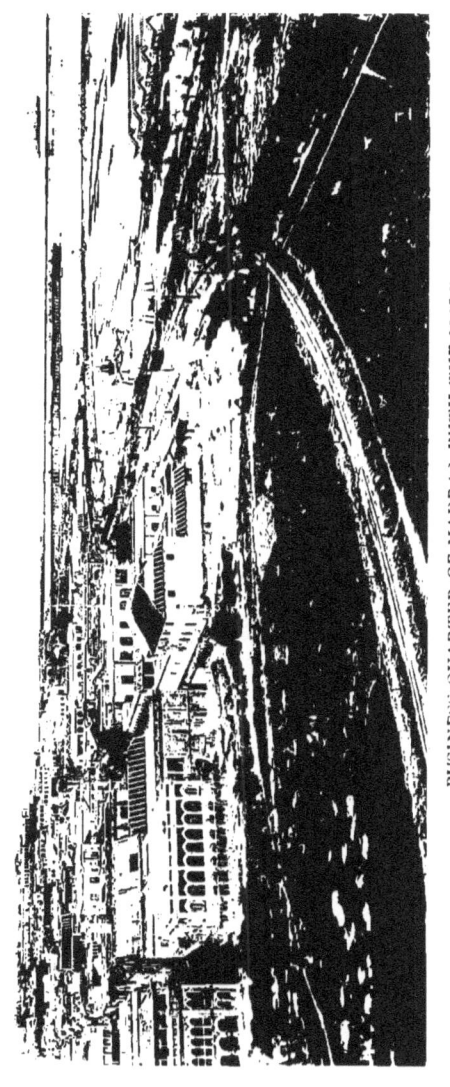

BUSINESS QUARTER OF MADRAS, WITH THE MOLE.

chosen for the capital and leading port of Southern India.

Madras has no natural harbor whatever, and the present abortive breakwater, forming a haven of about a thousand square yards, was only commenced within ten years. Even before the work was entirely completed, a tempest wrenched many of the gigantic blocks of concrete from their places, and opened great breaches in the walls.

As no attempt had been made to repair this disaster, the basin was of little avail against the high seas. Judging by a glance, it will be difficult to erect any barrier that will long withstand the violent elements of destruction.

Once inside, the ship was a centre for the deep Masulah boats, each manned by twelve nude, swarthy natives, and steered by a long oar. They are constructed without a single nail, threads of coir (cocoanut fibre) being used to sew the planks together. As one of these surged up to the steamer's gangway, threatening to dash itself to pieces, we threw in our traps and jumped aboard.

After making all reasonable effort to crash some of the other boats, involving the exchange of volumes of wordy abuse, our crew headed for the shore. One by one the billows overtook us, lifting our craft on high like a cork and dropping it again amid a shower of spray.

Cargo is mostly received by the lighters and discharged at a long pier, not unlike those at Long Branch and Brighton; but for landing humanity preference is given to beaching. We were now about to undergo this exciting ordeal.

Upon nearing the huge breakers the oarsmen braced themselves and pulled like Trojans, crying out in chorus to stimulate each other. Borne upon one foaming crest after another, in a moment the boat was safely resting on the sand. Then came the inevitable coolies, clad in a three-inch strip of muslin, to carry us upon their tawny shoulders beyond the reach of the waves.

Madras, with much more propriety than Washington, might be called a city of "magnificent distances." With a population of four hundred thousand souls, its disjointed length extends for nine miles along the sandy, torrid coast. The ethnographic divisions common to India are represented in its area of nearly thirty square miles.

First, Black Town and its dependencies, practically the Hindu quarter, but fronted towards the sea by public offices and business warehouses. This neighborhood contains the principal temple and the Evening Bazaar, where the natives gather late in the afternoon for petty traffic or to chat with their friends.

Next, Fort St. George, which stands on a stretch of green, and the adjacent Senate House and Government Mansion, with their gardens. Here we find a statue of Lord Cornwallis, who was Governor-General of India after his little mishap at Yorktown. He achieved better success with Tippoo Sahib and his sons, in the Mysore war, than with Washington and Lafayette. Extending southward from this vicinity is the foreign section, of which the main street is called Mount Road. The shops, like the yellow bungalows, are set each in its own compound. Lastly, we come to Triplicane and Chepauk, unsavory districts inhabited by seventy-five thousand Mohammedans.

Madras was founded by the East India Company as early as 1638, but its history is destitute of interest. For a century past it has recorded no event of political importance. Indeed, considering its size and position as a presidency capital, it is a conspicuously inert and featureless city.

The climate is hot, feverish, and oppressive during the greater part of the year, driving the government and wealthy residents to the hill resort of Ootacamund or else to Bangalore. Even in the coolest months the mid-day heat is intense, with heavy dews in the morning, but towards evening it moderates enough to invite a drive along the beach road. Added to these drawbacks, the coast is subject to the destructive hurricanes which sweep the Bay of Bengal in both the summer and winter monsoons.

Madras has direct railway communication with Bombay, and almost to the extremity of the peninsula, as well as a circuitous route to Calcutta. Along the southern line and its branches are most of the great Hindu pagodas and rock temples,—Madura, Trichinopoly, Tanjore, Conjeveram, and others,—marvels of barbaric workmanship and intricate carving.

Here the devotion to Vishnu and Siva is more bigoted than in the north, and to it is joined a belief in evil spirits, known as "devil worship." The people are of the Dravidian family, speaking the Tamil, Canarese, Telugu, and Malayalam languages. Their color is darker than that of the Aryans, or Indo-Europeans, but in common with that race it is supposed they originally came from beyond the Himalayas.

FAÇADE OF A DRAVIDIAN TEMPLE, TRICHINOPOLY.

CHAPTER XI.

CEYLON, THE PEARL.

Where the tints of the earth, and the hues of the sky,
In color though varied, in beauty may vie,
And the purple of Ocean is deepest in dye.
* * * * * * *
'Tis the clime of the East; 'tis the land of the Sun!
BYRON.

UPON leaving Madras another of the stanch Masulah boats carried us out to where the ship lay at anchor. More than the usual high sea was running, sufficient almost to clear the exposed harbor of small craft. But to this there was an amusing exception in the form of the native catamaran, not yet described.

The catamaran consists of three pieces of timber, bound together, the middle one being the longest and curved up at the fore like a prow. Upon this raft a solitary man paddles about, bidding defiance to wave and weather. If swept off by a mighty billow he is back again in a moment, and without any wet clothing to lament. Some of them, however, do have a small item of apparel, as the following incident will prove.

Just as the steamer was about to move, one of these amphibious creatures hurriedly approached with a delayed message from the company's agent. As he came nearer we began to wonder where he carried the paper, as both he and the catamaran were drenched at every surge. The mystery was soon explained. When close to the gangway he arose, took the letter from a strip of muslin wound about his head and placed it between his teeth. Then, unwinding this slight turban, which was really his dress suit, he deftly adjusted it about his loins and stepped on board with the confidence of a man properly attired.

The sea! the sea! again at sea even though we love it not. Now we headed southward, along the Coromandel Coast, passing the town of Pondicherry, one of the few in the peninsula which still acknowledge French supremacy.

On the second day we sighted the hills of Ceylon, "the resplendent," but without experiencing the "spicy breezes" of poetic fancy. Steaming around the eastern side of the island, on the third morning we anchored in the picturesque haven of Point de Galle.

As in all Oriental ports, the ship at once became the magnet for a miniature flotilla; but what curious boats! Imagine a double-ender thirty feet long and only sixteen inches wide, made of a hollowed trunk on the top of which boards are sewn to give it a depth of about a yard. Resting upon the water parallel with the canoe, and of nearly the same length, is an outrigger in the shape of a cylindrical log with pointed ends. The two are connected by a pair of curved poles, stretching across an interval of several feet. In sailing, the side thus weighted is always placed to the windward. No nails are used in the construction of these "double canoes," yet they are strong enough to venture out five leagues or more.

Before us, across the blue water, lay a quaint town, set amid a luxuriant, undulating landscape clad with numberless palms. Grouped in the distance the purple hills rose against the fervid azure, while a wealth of sunshine and balmy winter breezes lent their share to the conviction that this was indeed Ceylon,—"a pearl-drop on the brow of Ind."

Well may the antiquary suspect that here is the Tarshish from which Solomon brought his stores of ivory and apes, rare woods and precious stones.

Once ashore, the intense heat reminded us that we were now only six degrees north of the equator. The gauziest clothing afforded no relief in an atmosphere so charged with humidity. Everybody was suffering from continuous perspiration, and yet this is the cool season. At midday the narrow streets were deserted, but as the sun declined the people came forth, in general neatly dressed. Their estate in life is perceptibly better than that of the Indian masses, and Christianity has made more progress among them.

The Singalese of the coast are an effeminate race, having long hair twisted into a knot at the back and but little beard. Across the crown of the head they wear a semicircular comb, precisely like that formerly used by our young girls, its exact position depending upon the social grade of the individual. That even worldly caste should exist among the Singalese, who are devout Buddhists, is a perversion or a remnant of Brahminism, as the founder of the reformed faith expressly rejected such distinctions.

"Thus the World-honored spake: 'Pity and need
Make all flesh kin. There is no caste in blood,
Which runneth of one hue, nor caste in tears,
Which trickle salt with all; neither comes man

> To birth with tilka-mark stamped on the brow,
> Nor sacred thread on neck. Who doth right deeds
> Is twice-born, and who doth ill deeds vile.' "

The Tamils of Ceylon, who number about six hundred thousand, out of a total population of more than two and a half millions, are Hindus, like their brethren of Southern India. Another prominent class, though counting less than two hundred thousand, are the Moors. They comprise the shopkeepers, hawkers of curios, and dealers in precious stones, tortoise-shell, and ebony-ware. Persistent and careless of rebuffs, they haunt the hotels, solicit from their door-ways, and otherwise pester travellers. Their prices are as elastic as their consciences, and many of them show no hesitation in offering spurious gems.

Ceylon is the land of the ruby and the sapphire, the chrysoberyl (cat's-eye) and the pearl, but only a connoisseur can buy them here with safety.

The name Point de Galle, or Punto Gallo (Cock's Point), is a relic of the Portuguese occupation (1518-1658), and after them came the Dutch (1658-1796), who built the ramparts yet remaining. Following the English conquest, which occurred during a war with Holland, internal disturbances finally led to the dethronement (1815) of the native King of Kandy, and since that event the island has belonged solely to Great Britain.

Late one afternoon we took a Ceylon *bandy*, virtually a pony phaeton with a standing top and four seats, and went out to Wakwalla. The drive is locally noted for its beauty, which we fully realized. On both sides, the road is closely fringed with palms of several species, overhung with flowing creepers and relieved at intervals by white villages. The soil is of a bright ruddy color, owing to the presence of laterite rock. A more purely tropical picture I have never seen. From the porch of the bungalow at Wakwalla, located on an eminence, there is a charming view of wooded hills and valleys decked with exuberant vegetation.

Returning homeward, we stopped at one of the cinnamon gardens for which the place is famous. The plant grows to a height of six feet or more, and commences to yield the spicy bark about the seventh year. Contrary to the supposition inspired by such writers as Milton and Moore, there is no odor from the growing cinnamon.

Among the most dismal of a traveller's tasks is to start before daylight. Yet this he must endure for the privilege of taking Her Majesty's mail stage from Galle to Colombo, a distance of seventy miles. Or rather, from Galle to Kalutara, at which point a railway commences. Much to the discredit of the crown, we were kept waiting a doleful half-hour beyond the designated time.

In the struggle to occupy the interim, I climbed the old Dutch wall, over the street from the hotel, bent on a lesson in astronomy. The cloudless sky was favorable, and I easily placed two or three constellations not visible at home. There was the Southern Cross, riding high in the heavens. Four brightish stars form the figure with some accuracy, but a superfluous fifth, located almost on a line between the foot and the end of the right arm, detracts from the effect. If the truth be confessed, the Cross is rather insignificant and disappointing. It certainly fails to justify Dante in his sympathy for the peoples deprived of its radiance.

Turning to the north, I could barely distinguish the Polar Star through the haze which hung close to the horizon. Then I thought of the elevation at which I had seen it from the peaks of Norway, and was fast drifting into a revery when the rattling stage emerged from the darkness.

Her Majesty's mail was a sort of Germantown wagon, with extra places and a boot for luggage in the rear. A sudden crack of the whip started the four ponies, but not the stage, so we had another delay of fifteen minutes to repair the broken harness. At last we were off, dashing down the street and through the venerable town-gate, as if Tam O'Shanter's goblins were in pursuit.

A syce, or groom, who hung to the trap by a step, frequently jumped off and assisted the driver by lashing the little nags. The same active functionary also wound the horn, to clear the way and advise chance passengers in the villages of our coming.

Rosy dawn, and in the tropics! Who welcomes it not in every clime, unless it be an enthusiastic writer whom it detects still at work? It streamed into the coach and painted the flowers and verdure by the wayside. It revealed to us the wealth of surrounding Nature. The smooth, level road winding out from palm forests to the edge of the rippling sea, and back again.

On one side, the rocky headlands, the double canoes in the little harbors, the fishermen drawing their seines, and the gigantic saurian (iguana) crawling to its retreat. On the other, phalanx after phalanx of Ceylon's twenty million palms, the clustering cocoanuts, the nutmegs and the splendid orchids, the dusky peasantry, the chanting schools, and the rustic *pahndals* (triumphal arches) for some holy festival.

Words utterly fail to convey the pleasure which a traveller gleans from such a journey. In comparison with it a banquet with the costliest wines is stale, the grandest ball of the season flat, and lounging at summer resorts unprofitable.

There was but one foreigner on the stage besides ourselves, and he sat at the front with the driver. Opposite us inside, where we had the choice seats, were three of the better class of Singalese, all cleanly arrayed in their best. Not a word escaped from any of the trio during the whole six hours, but a small, matronly woman, who had the middle place, amused us by her bearing.

The people of Ceylon, like those of all tropical Asiatic countries, constantly chew a mixture of the peppery betel-leaf, the areca-nut, and a trifle of lime, which has an exhilarating effect and stains their teeth almost as red as blood. Now, our little woman was vigorously engaged in this soothing occupation, but as it has a tendency to create saliva, the accumulation gave her trouble. As she was entirely too proper to lean over the man on either side to make a discharge, it taxed her capacity to the utmost before a relay station, where all usually alighted, afforded a chance of relief. In the meanwhile, her lips were compressed and the utmost dignity prevailed.

The ponies were changed several times, in view of the terrific pace they are called upon to sustain. On two occasions they refused to start until the leaders' ears were nearly twisted off by rope tourniquets, and all four horribly beaten.

At Bentota, which overlooks the sea, where we had a late breakfast, or tiffin, they offered us the oysters for which the place is famous in Ceylon. They were diminutive, coppery, and inferior to the American species. In this vicinity, but some miles inland, is Ratnapura, the "city of gems," about which rubies, sapphires, and other precious stones are found.

We reached Kalutara at noon, and thence went by train—nearly thirty miles—to Colombo, the capital and metropolis of Ceylon.

Colombo, formerly called Kalambu, was so renamed by the Portuguese in honor of the discoverer of America. The better parts of the city are European in aspect, with modifications suited to a torrid climate. Many of the streets show their Dutch origin, and some have the sidewalks elevated a yard or more above the roadway. The Black Town, chiefly peopled by Singalese and Tamils, has the usual detail of a native quarter.

Considering that its population numbers over a hundred thousand, Colombo displays little outward activity. Its business thoroughfares are habitually quiet, and at mid-day almost deserted. The heat is extremely oppressive at all seasons; not as the result of a remarkably high temperature, but because of the great humidity of the atmosphere. In the shade the mercury seldom rises above ninety degrees, while the yearly average is a trifle over eighty.

Towards evening a refreshing breeze generally comes from the sea, when the foreign residents emerge from their suburban bungalows for a drive along the strand, known as the Galle Face, or else around the lake and out to the Cinnamon Gardens. Another favorite resort, dignified as Mount Lavinia, is a lone eminence, crowned by a hotel, situated directly on the shore, about seven miles south of the city.

From the balcony of our hotel in the Fort, a section once enclosed by massive Dutch battlements, we had a partial view of the harbor and the growing breakwater. Recognizing the value and necessity of a more secure anchorage, the government has expended a large sum upon the works. The intention is to centralize the island's commerce at the capital. Both of the leading steamship companies have erected new office buildings, and since our visit Colombo has become the mail port, instead of Galle.

There are no Buddhist temples of note within the city, and only one of the Hindu faith, which is conspicuous for its grotesque decoration. Here, as well as at Galle, travellers are tortured by dealers in precious stones, tortoise-shell, ebony-ware, and canes of the rich palm woods. The strength of our resolution to abstain from buying these things was represented by two boxes, despatched to New York by an American bark.

Colombo is a centre for the preparation of cocoanut oil, coir, and coffee. Of these three prominent staples of Ceylon, the last is the most important. Fifty years ago coffee was a trifling product, but the amount now annually exported varies from thirty to forty thousand tons, valued at fifteen to twenty million dollars. We visited one of the establishments where the raw coffee is received from the plantations to be cured for shipment. Most of the hands are Tamil women. The process, briefly, consists of drying the beans, shelling them by means of rollers, winnowing, sorting the berries by sieves of different meshes, and finally the packing in stout bags.

When cholera and its attendant quarantine forced us to abandon the trip to Bagdad, we lost a chance of seeing the pearl fisheries of the Persian Gulf. Here again, in Ceylon, we were fated to miss the same coveted sight.

The location of the pearl banks is the bay of Condatchy, less than a hundred and fifty miles north of Colombo. Despite the magnitude of this interest, which is a State monopoly, no town of any extent marks the favored vicinity, and the surrounding landscape is parched, flat, and inhospitable. Yet when it is announced, after an official inspection, that fishing will be permitted during certain months, usually in the spring, the lifeless place becomes all animation. A numerous fleet of boats gathers from the neighboring coasts, a multitude of natives come from the interior, and a great camp of palm huts is quickly constructed.

At a given signal, that all may fare equally well, the exciting work begins. Hundreds of divers, ready with their sinking-stones, ropes, and baskets, instantly plunge into the sea. After a time they reappear, breathless from the long immersion, with their baskets full of the peculiar mollusks which bear the precious gems. Then another set descend into the depths, each craft having several, and so on till the boats are laden. The divers are sometimes attacked by sharks and obliged to use their knives in defence.

When the oysters are landed a division is made. The boatmen receive either a third or a fourth as their share, and the government takes the remainder. Those belonging to the colony are at once disposed of by auction, in lots of a thousand.

The result of these sales is, of course, an assured revenue. But such is not the position of the buyer. His purchase is distinctly a speculation. There is no certainty that it will yield in pearls enough to exceed the amount of his outlay. He could bid for unclaimed express packages with equal doubt of profit. A hundred oysters may not contain a solitary pearl, and yet two or three are sometimes found in one shell.

The mollusks are allowed to putrefy in the burning sun, and are then carefully washed to extract the dainty jewels from the foul dross. During this odorous process the owner must be ever vigilant, or his workmen will relieve him of the choicest treasures. In truth, pearl-fishing, like mining for diamonds or gold, is for all concerned a precarious occupation.

From Colombo we went by rail to Kandy, the virtual capital of Ceylon, situated in the mountain region of the interior. The colonial governor usually resides there, as the atmosphere is drier and the temperature cooler than on the coast. Like sundry other railways, the one to Kandy, seventy-five miles long, is claimed to be the most profitable in the world. It also has the woful distinction of having caused the death of a coolie for every sleeper in its construction. The fevers of the jungles through which it passes are almost as deadly as those of the swamps along the Panama line.

Once outside of Colombo, the train dashes into dense tropical forests and over a flat country marked with miniature lakes and verdant fields of paddy. Throughout the route prolific vegetation is struggling to recover the pathway cleared for the rails. Here and there a monkey swings from tree to tree, but to see his kind in troops we must penetrate to the undisturbed domain of nature.

After the first thirty miles the road begins to ascend. We at once experienced a relief from the saturating heat, which was thankfully appreciated. Amid charming scenery we wound upward, around the slopes of steep, wooded hills, and close to the edge of jutting cliffs. Low down in the teeming glens and valleys much of the ground is cunningly terraced for growing rice, the falling water dripping from step to step over the brilliant green.

At intervals in the exuberant foliage the eye singled out the stately talipot palm, with its great feathery flower rising grandly in the centre above the topmost leaves. It was our rare fortune to see a number of these trees in bloom.

Once we had a glimpse of Adam's Peak (7350 feet), the sacred mountain of Ceylon. A Buddhist shrine crowns its craggy summit, where an artificial outline in the rock, five feet long, is declared by the credulous to be a human footprint. The Buddhists attribute it to Gautama, the Brahmins to Siva, and the Muslims to Adam.

According to the myth of the local Muslims, Adam lived several years on this mount, apart from his wife, after the exile from Eden. During this period Eve was at Jeddah, where her lengthy tomb is located. Before her death she was reunited to Adam on Mount Arafat, near Mecca, after a separation of one hundred and twenty years.

Higher up we enter the coffee belt, passing at first some abandoned plantations. Attempts to cultivate the Arabian berry below an elevation of about a thousand feet, generally thus end in failure. A medium level, say three thousand feet, is the best. On the contrary, the Liberian species, of which, however, there is but little raised in Ceylon, flourishes from a height of two thousand feet down to the sea. The great coffee district of the island is around Gampola, which is reached by a branch line from the railway to Kandy.

Here, also, we see splendid clumps of bamboo, striking ferns and orchids, and satin-wood, ebony, and bread-fruit trees. The last recalls the inimitable comic description by Dr. Holmes, in the "Autocrat at the Breakfast Table":

"The bread-fruit tree grows abundantly. Its branches are well known to Europe and America under the familiar name of *macaroni*. The smaller twigs are called *vermicelli*. . . . The fruit of the bread-tree consists principally of hot rolls. The buttered muffin variety is supposed to be a hybrid with the cocoanut palm, the cream found in the milk of the cocoanut exuding from the hybrid in the shape of butter, just as the ripe fruit is splitting."

When the train halted at a station, the olive-brown Singalese came to sell us plantains and fresh young cocoanuts. With a sudden stroke of a heavy knife, they cut through the soft green husk and yet unhardened shell of the nut, to offer the cool milk to their customers. The natives and many foreigners think it a refreshing drink, but we found it too sweet and cloying, and the slight, tender kernel was insipid. We saw little of the matured fruit, like that sold in America.

The cocoa palm bears from about the seventh to the seventieth year of its life, after which it is felled and utilized for a legion of purposes. Under native care the annual product of a tree is from thirty to fifty nuts, but on plantations managed by Europeans the average is much higher. While the fruit is ripening, which requires twelve months, one of the long palm leaves is commonly tied, spear to spear, about the trunk. As this soon dries, it warns the owner by crackling if a midnight thief attempts to climb the tree,—not an unusual occurrence.

It would be difficult to enumerate the many and varied uses of the cocoanut palm. From the juice of the blossom and of the fruit the Singalese makes his toddy; the milk of the nut is his beverage; and the kernel, besides the valuable oil it yields, is prominent as an article of diet. Even the refuse from the oil-presses serves as food for his poultry and cattle, and, when partly decomposed, as manure for the very trees from which it came.

The husks are his fuel, the shells his vessels, and in the coir he finds a suitable fibre for his ropes and nets. The leaves provide him with dishes, a roof above his head, and a shelter from the sun; while a slip of the bark acts as a simple bolt. After all this array there is still the trunk, which furnishes material for his house, his furniture, domestic utensils, fences, boats, and, lastly, his coffin.

By this time we have passed Bible Rock, so named from its likeness to a book open upon a cushion; and Sensation Rock, which threatens to hurl its beetling mass down upon the daring train. Soon we reach the summit of the pass; stop a moment at the euphonious Peradeniya, and then descend slightly to Kandy, alighting just as the sheen of sunset is tinting the highland capital.

Kandy is one of the most picturesque of towns, nestling "among the many-folded hills," a bright gem in a rich setting. A long, ornate lake, partly natural and partly artificial, located on the edge of the European quarter, adds greatly to the inherent beauty of the picture. Here the Singalese kings held their courts before the coming of the foreigner, and here for centuries has stood a central shrine of the Buddhist faith.

The country in the vicinity of Kandy affords glorious drives and walks over good roads, and fronting the modest hotel is a pretty open green. Among other places we drove to the botanical gardens of Peradeniya, three miles distant. There, in addition to a fine display of palms, we found some notable specimens of the India-rubber tree. The straight, branching roots, lifting their ridges six or eight feet above the ground, extend several yards in every direction.

About a day's journey from Kandy by rail and coach, through the coffee district and a scenic country, lies a beautiful sanitarium called Nuwara Eliya. Its situation, close to Pedrotallagalla, the highest mountain of the island, having an elevation of eight thousand three hundred feet, gives it a moderate climate even in the hottest months. There exhausted Europeans retire to recuperate, often to avoid the necessity of a trip home.

North of the centre of the island are the ruins of the two ancient capitals, Anuradhapura and Polonaruwa. The remains consist of Buddhist tanks, palaces, tombs, and temples, some of which

TEMPLE OF THE SACRED TOOTH, KANDY.

antedate the Christian era. At the former is a venerable Bo-tree, reputed the oldest (B.C. 288) of any kind in the world. There is likewise reason to believe that it was raised from a branch of the sacred Tree of Wisdom, at Gaya, in India, under which Prince Siddartha, or Gautama, experienced the mental struggle by which he attained Buddhahood.

In consequence of this vital element of their creed, which might be likened to the Forty Days' Temptation, Buddhists regard the Bo-tree much as Christians do the Cross. Hence one is planted close to a temple. It belongs to the Indian fig species, its technical name being *Ficus religiosa*, and somewhat resembles the banian.

The leaves of this tree are hung by so slight a stem that the least breeze causes them to vibrate, which at once arrests the attention. This peculiarity has duly received a mythical interpretation. They are said to tremble in remembrance of Gautama's conflict with the spirits of evil under their branches,—like those of the aspen, of which tradition has built the Cross, in token of the sacrifice on Calvary.

The object of supreme interest in Kandy is the Temple of the Dalada, where the celebrated tooth of Buddha is enshrined. In contrast with Hinduism, and contrary to the teachings of Gautama, the Buddhist system, as now perverted, recognizes the worship of relics. Around this sanctuary—the Mount Athos or St. Peter's of the Southern Buddhists—the hierarchy has gathered, and devout pilgrims visit it from the most distant parts of Asia. Standing within its portals, we could not but think that more than a third of the human race piously envied our privilege.

So complicated is the plan of the temple, with an adjoining palace, that I could scarcely make a description clear or entertaining. The buildings and the enclosing walls are of stone, and massively constructed. A conspicuous feature of the pile is a low, octagon tower, encircled by a balcony, which overlooks the green. This contains a revered collection of Pali manuscripts, and the Three Pitakas, or Buddhist scriptures, written on wood and bound as folios. Palm-leaves are also used, but printing has never been employed.

For more than three hundred years after the death of Gautama his precepts were not even reduced to writing. "The wise monks of former days," says the record, as quoted by Rhys Davids, "handed down by word of mouth the text of the Three Pitakas and the Commentary upon them;

seeing the destruction of men the monks of this time (about B.C. 80) assembled, and, that the truth might last long, they wrote them in books."

Mounting a dingy flight of steps, we pass through a sombre hall and enter the court of the temple. Here, amid the clashing of drums and of gongs, people of both sexes are chatting or else buying flowers for oblations. Under the guidance of a priest we are first conducted into a dark chapel, filled with kneeling worshippers. At the far end, screened by a glass partition and dimly lighted with candles, is a golden image of Buddha, as well as other paraphernalia of pagan rites.

The idol has the conventional attitude,—sitting with the legs crossed and the hands resting on the knees. On the face is that expression of peaceful, stainless, passive repose of one "who has conquered (sin) by means of holiness; from whose eyes the veil of error has been removed, and who, free from yearning, has attained Nirvana." Not as of a soul accepted in heaven, for Buddhist doctrine recognizes neither one nor the other, much less a ruling godhead.

Rather a state of perfect wisdom and celestial calm; a condition of personal inexistence, yet not of mental extinction; a relief from all that under the workings of Karma* would cause a perpetuation of life in some form, on the principle of transmigration. "While his body shall remain he will be seen by gods and men, but after the termination of life, upon the dissolution of the body, neither gods nor men will see him."

"All life is lived for him, all deaths are dead."

After a glance at the treasures of the library, before mentioned, we follow our guide into the hallowed sanctuary,—a small, square building, placed in the centre of the court. A short staircase leads up to a narrow room, crowded with prostrate devotees. The air in the apartment is hot, impure, and saturated with the odor of a flower like the tuberose.

Before us a pair of doors, inlaid with carved ivory, open at our approach, and we step into the contracted inmost chamber, the Holy of the Holies. Directly in front is a table loaded with the floral offerings of the devout, and behind it rise the strong iron bars of a cage. Inside this protection,

---

* This is the doctrine that, as soon as a sentient being dies, a new being is produced in a more or less painful and material state of existence, according to the "karma," the desert or merit, of the being who had died.—*Rhys Davids's "Buddhism."*

standing on a silver altar, is the shrine of the Dalada, or sacred tooth.

The reliquary, shaped like a bell and about four feet in height, is made of silver gilt, set with precious stones and decked with chains. Within this are five more cases, one beneath the other, of similar design. Upon removing the last the venerated object is exposed, resting upon a golden lotus.

The pretended history of the relic declares it to be the left eye-tooth of Buddha, which was taken from the ashes of his funeral pile (B.C. 543), at Kusinara. After being kept at Dantapura, in Southern India, for above seven hundred years, it was brought to Ceylon for better security, in the fourth century of our era. Later it was carried back to India by the invading Malabars; but Prakrama the Great (1153–1186) recovered it by force of arms. During the Portuguese occupation (1560) the Catholic missionaries removed it to Goa, south of Bombay, the centre of Portugal's Indian possession. There, after declining all offers of ransom, they ground the tooth to powder, every particle of which was carefully destroyed.

The record of this curious act is detailed and authentic. Yet the wily priests of Kandy, as soon as prudence would permit, announced that it was only a counterfeit which had thus suffered destruction. The genuine relic, as the Buddhists relate, was then produced and borne to the temple with great ceremony and rejoicing.

When the British came as conquerors, they took possession of the precious object for political effect. Besought by the devout Singalese, they gracefully restored it as an evidence of friendship and mutual confidence.

But a most extraordinary fact in connection with this momentous trifle remains to be stated; a reality so perplexing in its application to the eventful story that it forms a strange and fitting climax. In a word, the supposed tooth of Buddha never belonged in a human mouth. It measures two inches in length, and has the appearance of ordinary ivory. And yet before this spurious relic nearly five hundred millions of people are ready to prostrate themselves in profound adoration.

CHAPTER XII.

RARE EXPERIENCES.

> Happy is he who lives to understand
> Not human nature only, but explores
> All natures, to the end that he may find
> The law that governs each.
> WORDSWORTH.

WHEN we entered Kandy the town bore evidences of an approaching event. The streets and houses were decorated with flags and lanterns, and mottoes on transparencies extended a loyal welcome to princely guests. Around the public green deft hands were erecting an ornamental railing of bamboo and palm, with half a cocoanut upon each post to hold oil and wick for an illumination.

Upon inquiry we learned that Princes Albert Victor and George of Wales, then making a tour of the world as midshipmen on H. M. S. "Bacchante," were expected at Colombo on the following day. After a brief stay in that city they were coming to Kandy, to witness a representation of the great Buddhist feast of the Perahara.

Three days passed very pleasantly before the Princes came one afternoon by special train. When the booming of cannon announced their arrival, all was excitement and bustle. Both Europeans and natives gave them a hearty reception, as they drove from the station and through the town. Not far from the Government House a crowd of boisterous coffee-planters dashed at the equipage, detached the horses, and dragged the carriage to its destination, much to the astonishment of the occupants. Throughout this adventure, and during their entire stay, the bearing of the two young guests was modest and dignified.

That evening witnessed the Perahara, which proved the most weird and striking of all the spectacles of the East. This festival, which signifies "the procession," is the greatest in the calendar of the Ceylonese Buddhists, and is given in homage to the Dalada, or sacred tooth. It occurs yearly, and properly in July, culminating at full moon with the pageant by which it is chiefly known.

After the parade certain priests perform the rite of cutting the waters of the Mahawilla Ganga, the principal river of the island. Embarking in ornamental canoes they await the coming of dawn, and at that moment describe a circle in the stream with

GROUP OF SINGALESE CHIEFS, KANDY.

golden swords, and from within the imaginary space thus sanctified they fill vessels and bear the water to the temple.

At rare intervals a special representation of the Perahara is given, without regard to season, in honor of an exalted visitor, as in the case of the Prince of Wales (1875). The coming of his two sons was now made the occasion for a similar repetition in the winter months. Since the final deposition of the Kandyan kings the regular celebration has lost much of its earlier pomp and state, owing to the lack of the sacred presence of the monarch. But in this instance extensive preparations had been perfected to restore the ceremonial and splendor which formerly marked the Perahara.

Head-men and officials of the colony had been exerting themselves to the utmost for several days. A number of enormous elephants, some from distant points, were in readiness, together with their gorgeous paraphernalia and followers. Natives of distinction, in their robes of office, and devil-dancers from neighboring temples, all in strange costumes, were gathered with Buddhist priests, torch-bearers, stilt-walkers, tom-tom beaters, fifers, and men dressed in imitation of huge birds.

At the hotel a strong delegation of coffee-planters

took complete possession, and enjoyed themselves in the roughest, noisiest manner. Although extra tables were provided for the rush, they occupied every seat and turned the dinner into a wild orgie. They drank deeply, shouted, threw things about, and wrenched the food from the hands of servants. If a waiter approached with a roast pig, it was taken from him in an instant and torn to pieces by savage hands.

Toward the close of the revel the floor and tables presented the appearance of a sty, and maudlin acts and language were rampant. Dishes and glass were crashed, with empty bottles as a hammer, chairs overturned, and the pantry and bar invaded. At the end, when the national air was sung, many stood on the chairs and stamped time with a foot on the wreck of the feast, until one long table was crushed to the reeking floor.

All night through ribald profanity ruled the house, and sleep was impossible. Happily, nowhere, before nor since, have we seen another assemblage of Englishmen so disgrace the Queen and their country.

After nightfall the town was gayly illuminated and thousands crowded the streets. The cumbrous procession slowly formed in the open space fronting the temple, amid much confusion and chattering. When the line was at length in order, a gun was fired as the signal to start. Instantly there arose a deafening clangor of bells, cymbals, reeds, tomtoms, and voices.

First came a band of these supposed musicians, and after them three monster elephants, the middle one a noble tusker. All were gaudily caparisoned, but the one was specially honored by bearing the miniature temple which contains the sacred tooth, when the Perahara is legitimately celebrated.

A group of devil-dancers followed, all clad so fantastically as to baffle description. Some wore short skirts of bright colors, like ballet-girls, with a profusion of jingling trinkets; and others, suits covered with shrill bells or small dangling plates of silver. Thus prepared for noise, they flung themselves into every conceivable posture, turning somersaults, performing pirouettes and acrobatic feats, gyrating, dancing, and vaulting.

This peculiar function was executed with tireless and frantic zeal, as if each performer must outdo his fellows. In the popular worship these devil-priests are believed to have power, through their dancing and incantations, to exorcise demons, in case of illness or a threatened calamity.

After the devil-dancers marched a body of headmen, or native chiefs, whose costumes attracted every eye. The body of the dress was of scarlet, white, and gold, puffed out far beyond the natural size and decorated with chains, medals, and daggers. Hose of colored silk, curious shoes, and a four-cornered hat of unexampled model, completed the figure. Among them were men with snowy beards, and one was so aged as to require assistance in walking.

Next came more elephants, the howdahs filled with natives carrying lofty fans, golden umbrellas, and characteristic standards. Other participants on foot likewise bore these emblems, as well as blazing torches and brilliant shields. Then, perhaps, among these gaudy trappings, appeared the simple yellow robe of Gautama's order of monks. Or the comical stilt-walkers and the tall, grotesque imitations of birds and human beings, made of bamboo and painted canvas.

So the memorable procession repeated itself, over and over again, until I had counted thirty-six elephants, and found it had been forty minutes in passing. Toward the conclusion a drizzling rain fell, which extinguished the failing cocoanut-oil lights, and by midnight effectually scattered the spectators.

PREPARING FOR THE HUNT.

The pandemonium in the hotel, before and after the Perahara, made us long for morning, when we took the first train back to Colombo. There we at once prepared to leave the same evening for the scene of the greatest adventure which our tour of the world developed.

While at Kandy we heard that a grand elephant-hunt had been projected for the young Princes, to take place immediately after the Perahara. In our desire to partake of so rare an experience, we communicated with the American Consul at Colombo, asking if horses or a conveyance could be procured to take us to the appointed spot, thirty miles in the interior of the island.

The result was that we engaged him personally, at a round price, to drive us there and back in his own private carriage. Much to our discomfort, at the last moment he found himself unable to provide more than one horse, which forced us to go in a small, open trap.

During the afternoon a heavy wagon was sent ahead with the camping equipment and a servant to prepare the palm huts, previously ordered for our party. At sundown we followed, burdened with little more than the hammocks for use that night. In addition to the driver and ourselves, a syce clung to a step on the rear axle, to act as groom and whip. As we cleared the town the sun dipped below the horizon, lighting the sky with a splendor which invoked a glad hosanna, best given voice by Metastasio:

> "I see Thee in Thy works,
> I meet Thee in my heart."

Our way led almost directly eastward, never far from the course of the Kalany Ganga, the stream which empties at Colombo. In many places the road was heavy from the recent rains, making our progress very slow, and in climbing hills charity for the poor horse required us to walk.

Fortunately, my place was on the back seat, so that I was relieved of much of the burden of conversation. Fatigue and loss of sleep had made me so drowsy, that several times I was in danger of dropping out of the trap. Twice my helmet fell in the mud, after a narrow escape of this kind. During a stage journey of forty-eight hours, coming from the Yellowstone Park to the railroad, I once lost two hats in the same manner.

Soon after midnight we halted at a wayside bungalow, to refresh ourselves and feed the horse. Here the compound was crowded with cattle and wagons, all bound in our direction. After fortifying ourselves with strong tea, in the hope of keeping awake, we again took the road. But it was a cheerless drive, too dark to see anything.

In the small hours we passed a habitation, but our conductor thought it better to press on to a known rest-house at Hanwella. When we eventually arrived there, it was only to find it closed. Another hour or more brought us upon a great congregation of vehicles and cattle, the point where the road ended.

Thence to the camp, one had either to be mounted or go afoot. But we had no idea of proceeding any farther at that moment. So we slung the hammocks in an open shed, and enjoyed the sleep of the tired.

Early in the morning, after a cup of tea, we began the walk through the jungle, as no horses had been provided for the purpose. However, as there were coolies to carry all encumbrances, the tramp through luxuriant tropical foliage, beside running brooks, was not without its attractions. The drawbacks were the slippery mud and the troublesome leeches which infest the undergrowth of Ceylon. To guard against these parasites it is necessary to wear top-boots, or else wrap the trousers closely around the ankles down to the shoes.

Upon arriving at Kraaltown, for so the camp was called, we were at once installed in our quarters. The huts formed part of one of several rows, erected in conjunction with a dining-room as an improvised hotel. All were built of branches, thatched with palm leaves, and inside there was nothing except a bench of the same material extending around the wall, for sitting and sleeping. Other requisite furniture had been provided in our outfit.

Here, on the bank of a stream, directly in the damp, unhealthy jungle, we remained three days, but happily without injurious results, probably owing to the use of quinine as a prophylactic. The motionless, heated air was replete with moisture, and at short intervals heavy showers made everything wet and uncomfortable. Walking was a plague, on account of the mud, leeches, and sultriness, and at night we slept under open umbrellas, as rain freely came through the light thatch.

On a hill, a short distance from our quarters, neat cottages of palm-wood had been prepared for the Princes, the governor of the island, and the admiral of the fleet. These were furnished and curtained in the cosiest manner, including even the luxury of cots. The remainder of the camp, which was planned with some regularity, consisted of huts

ENTRANCE TO THE KRAAL.

like our own, many detached and others in rows. On the outskirts were the sutlers' booths, and that institution which alone advances with perfect security to the extreme frontiers of civilization—the bar.

The ground chosen for the exciting sport was a narrow valley close to the Labugama water-works, by which Colombo—thirty miles distant—is to be supplied. A locality known to be frequented by elephants is selected; one where the needful water, shade, and forage are present.

In such a spot the kraal had been erected by the natives, under the direction of their chiefs. This popular term is a heritage from the Dutch occupation, and corresponds to our word corral. As the cut shows, it formed an irregular figure, but not unlike a square with one corner truncated. The matter of outline, however, is governed somewhat by the topography of the site. It may describe a rectangle or a triangle, but must always have the added funnel, marked "Fence," to lead the herd to the entrance. Care must also be taken not to destroy the foliage about the approach to the trap, as the elephant has a keen instinct of danger.

The enclosure is constructed of the trunks of trees, nearly a foot in diameter and firmly set in the ground, crossed with rails of lesser thickness, and usually braced from the outside with forked timbers. In place of western modes of joining, the

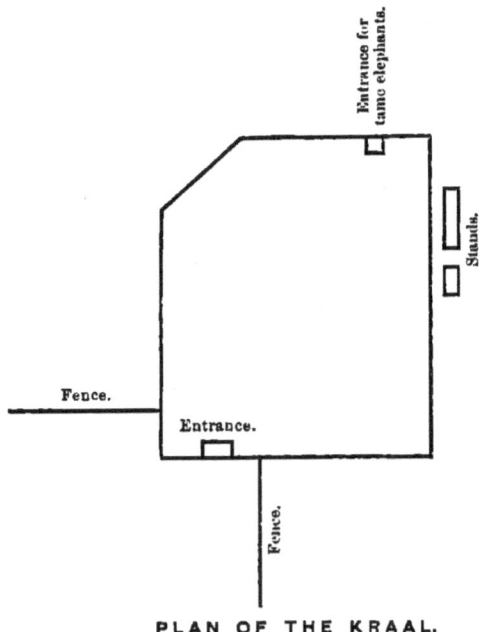

PLAN OF THE KRAAL.

parts are lashed with rattan and other stout tendrils, known as jungle ropes.

The whole covered a space of some three acres, and had a height of about ten feet. Adjoining the kraal were stands for the distinguished guests and visitors from all parts of the island, to view the operation of fettering the captives.

Despite its strength, such a barrier would be futile were an enraged elephant allowed to attack it with all his power. This contingency is generally prevented by stratagem; but at times it occurs, when the escape of the herd is probable. The devices employed to ward off a charge are of the simplest character, never implying force, but always depending upon man's craft and daring, and the timorous nature of the giant brute.

After the kraal had been completed, nearly three thousand natives were engaged for several weeks in securing the game. A large section of country was surrounded, and the cordon slowly contracted until about twenty elephants, comprising two distinct herds, were brought within surveillance. One chief declared that he had driven his herd eighty miles.

In pursuing this work of patience, tact, and hardship, the beaters are cautious not to alarm the elephants, but to allow them, as much as possible, to pursue their usual, peaceful habits in the jungle, at the same time advancing them, step by step, day and night, in the direction of the stockade.

When the circle has been so reduced as to excite

their mistrust, or the danger of a stampede, fires are built at close intervals around the line, and the watchers flash torches, brandish light spears, or sound a cry known to be hideous to the elephantine ear, "Harri-harri-hooi-ooi!"

Such were the extensive preparations when, one afternoon, the heir presumptive of the British Empire and his brother rode into Kraaltown, attended by officials, coffee-planters, and knots of dark-hued natives. Close by the corral were twenty monarchs of the forest, summoned to entertain the sea princes by yielding their liberty with struggles befitting a mighty race. And here were we from an antipodal home, like "marks of interrogation wandering up and down the world," waiting in the jungles of Ceylon to acquire new experiences by studying exotic natures. Can any philosophy lower than Fontenelle's account for so unwonted a grouping, in a more unwonted spot? "La véritable philosophie s'élève jusqu'à dévenir une espèce de théologie."

Sunset was upon the camp before the stir caused by the arrival of the Princes had subsided, and then word came that the "drive-in" would not be attempted until the following morning. After dinner some veterans of Indian life amused us for an hour or more with stories of elephants, tigers, leopards, and snakes, before we retired to the rude couches to dream of encounters with savage creatures. But it was not all a dream.

Shortly before daylight, when the prattling Singalese outside made it impossible to sleep, there fell upon our ears the most appalling cry of terror that a human being could utter. In an instant we were upon our feet. Its piercing tone of despair roused the occupants of every hut, and a moment later the ominous word "cobra" flew from tongue to tongue. Men clad in pajamas and slippers, followed by excited natives, dashed to the rescue,—to find that a partition of light palm leaves had fallen on the slumbering victim of fright. The incident was serious enough, however, to prove the animated respect which "old Indians" have for the imperious serpent.

After this adventure we had the early tea and prepared for the bugle-call, the signal that the great spectacle of the day was about to commence. Morning passed, but without the expected summons. To occupy the time and learn the cause of the delay, we walked over the hills to the rear of the kraal, only to hear that the beaters were having difficulty in bringing the game to the entrance.

Here were stationed the large, tame elephants selected to assist in noosing their wild brethren. One of the number, an enormous tusker, equipped with chains and ropes, stood the ideal of strength and docility. Encouraged by his driver we fed him with sweet stalks, which were taken with the utmost grace, and in return he gently lifted us high into the air upon his tusks, using his trunk with almost human care to guard us against a fall.

The trained elephant is associated in the Occident with amusement only, but throughout the East Indies he serves various purposes of utility. In addition to his offices in war and pageantry, of which we have already had glimpses, he is valuable in constructing roads, moving heavy stones, uprooting small trees, clearing a jungle, hauling weighty loads, and piling timber.

Most observers agree that his power and sagacity are best displayed in the task of handling lumber. At the command of his mahout, emphasized by the prick of an iron goad, he will select a log among many,—weighing half a ton or more,—lift it upon his tusks, carry it to the required place, and return for another. Two working in conjunction will rear a pile with the greatest accuracy, arranging the logs in rows crossing each other at right angles.

ELEPHANTS HANDLING TIMBER.

As long as silence governed the plan of strategy, visitors were enjoined from going towards the front of the kraal; and this prohibition, added to the long delay, caused much outspoken impatience; but when, suddenly, a distant storm of cries and shrill noises announced that the "drive in" was imminent, and the need of concealment past, we hurried forward to an elevated position overlooking the entrance.

The hunted elephants, terrified by the uproar, bolted headlong to the open gate, halted there for a moment undecided, and then, suspecting the trap, turned again on their pursuers. An army of natives, reinforced by many European volunteers, retired without ceremony, but only a few rods; and then promptly reformed their lines. Advancing again, the beaters boldly pricked the infuriated, trumpeting monsters with the light wands they carried, at the same time wildly gesticulating and shouting "harri-harri." But the herd stood in close order, refusing to move forward.

A long and stirring contest now ensued, much of which was hidden from us by the tall jungle. Even when the combatants were invisible, the position of the elephants was indicated by the cracking bamboos, waving trees, stentorian growls, and sometimes an uplifted trunk. Under the leadership of a savage cow, bent upon protecting the calf at her side, they repeatedly charged the cordon, only to be driven back by harmless screams and toy spears. Finally, a native ventured too near the desperate mother, and in an instant she caught him with her trunk and crushed out his life with a mammoth foot.

It was now decided that the leader must be disabled, to curb her fury. After a short truce—until a rifle was brought—the gallant brute fell, wounded near the ear; and while her blood poured out in a great stream, the little calf ran about the prostrate form in appealing distress. The cow lay perhaps five minutes; then unexpectedly rose, gathered the herd about her, and led them with a rush through the funnel and into the enclosure. I saw every one of them pass the fence,—seven wild elephants; and in the flush of that moment I had scored a rare experience. In an instant watchers sprang forward and barred the entrance. At last the captives were "kraaled."

The instinct that two herds of elephants never mingle, was dominant even during the critical struggle; the larger body, yet outside, having succeeded in maintaining separate ground, and so, for a time, escaped capture. Hence the lines were continued with unabated vigilance around the herd still in the jungle, until the gate could be safely opened for another drive.

Contrary to all precedent, steps were immediately taken for "tying up" that afternoon. Usually a night is allowed to intervene, as the prisoners spend their rage and exhaust themselves in the interval by vain assaults upon the stockade, tearing through the heavy undergrowth, and bellowing in alarm and bewilderment. By morning they stand together, silent and subdued, and as far from their tormenters as possible.

This premature movement, undertaken against the advice of the chiefs, was ordered for the reason that the Princes were timed to leave that evening. Unwisely, only two days had been allotted in the reception programme for the kraal, and so the royal guests were hurried away to Nuwara Eliya for an elk-hunt, which proved a failure. Many visitors, however, remained until the end, including the admiral and some of his lieutenants.

Briefly, the too hasty attempt at noosing, executed in a deluge of rain, was unsuccessful; this, be it noted, in defiance of the herculean efforts of three tame elephants to butt and belabor the wild ones into subjection. As the wounded cow still gave battle, she was reluctantly killed during this fray, and the marksman proudly bore off the tail as his trophy.

Let us pass over the detail of how the corral was forced that night and the captives escaped. Also of how they were soon retaken, along with six from the other herd. In a word, when the "tying up" began in earnest there were twelve unfortunates in the toils.

The victims were engaged in cooling each other with mud and water when the bars of the small rear entrance were removed and four tame elephants entered, each mounted by two or three noosers, and followed by assistants with spears and ropes. In a trice the herd took fright and charged the palisade, only to retreat before the puny wands and loud whoops of the guards. Despairing of escape, they dashed to and fro, round and round, to avoid contact with the approaching foes. Thus pressed without respite, they sometimes evinced a disposition to be warlike, which was effectually checked by a few blows or thumps from the tame animals. In these encounters the exposed riders were unnoticed and unharmed, but the men on foot were cautious to evade attack.

FETTERED AND STRUGGLING.

After long manœuvring the trained elephants managed to separate a large cow from the herd, and so ranged themselves about her that she was forced to stand. This was the opportunity wanted, and in a flash an agile native slipped under one of the friendly brutes, rope in hand. Waiting until the restless prisoner lifted her hind foot, he deftly placed the noose about her leg and withdrew. Another venture fettered the second limb, the decoys meanwhile warding off with their trunks several wrathful strokes aimed at the man.

The ropes were now firmly secured to a stout tree, and the captive left entirely alone, save her calf. Then began a titanic struggle for liberty, that no few words can justly portray. Finding herself baffled in untying the many knots, or in uprooting the tree, she writhed, screamed, tore at the foliage, pawed the earth, tossed clouds of dust over her back, flung her trunk about fiercely, and planted her head upon the ground for leverage to rend asunder the bonds. At length she fell, in exhaustion, anguish, and despair, and lay motionless and resigned. The natives well knew that these symptoms forebode the loss of their prize. She panted for an hour or more, sighed deeply, and died—of "broken heart."

A male somewhat above medium size was next submitted to the exciting ordeal, with minor variations. While he stood jammed between two of the tame elephants, away from any tree, the nooser induced him to raise his hind foot by touching it gently, drew the running knot about his leg, and retreated. In this case the rope was attached to the girth of one of the trained animals, and the sagacious brute, knowing exactly what was expected of him, began to drag the captive towards a tree facing the spectators' stands. The wild one resisted violently, but without avail, as the tame allies steadily pushed, butted, and pulled him across the enclosure. When the tying was complete his contortions to free himself were astonishing, though in the end he calmed down, hopeless and covered with soil.

While these operations were in progress the two orphan calves became troublesome,—wailing, charging to and fro, chasing the noosers, and running under the grown elephants. As the element of danger was absent, the binding of these little ones was merry work. In addition to securing one leg, a noose was passed round their necks. They bellowed, threw off the ropes, rapped their assailants, and displayed the most comical exasperation.

NOOSING WILD ELEPHANTS.

Elephants with tusks are comparatively rare in Ceylon, but there was a huge one in the kraal, fifty or sixty years of age,—too old to be trained. Contrary to rule, he was the most cowardly of the herd, persistently declining to fight and always eluding his pursuers. The natives were indisposed seriously to attempt his capture, and even the tame beasts preferred to leave him undisturbed.

The process of training commences by giving the captive a small quantity of food, which is increased from day to day. At the expiration of a week or two, according to the individual temper, he is chained between tame elephants and led away to bathe. If patience and kindness be exercised, in two months his driver can ride him unattended, and in another similar period he is prepared for labor.

The work of "tying up" continued a second day, but few strangers cared to remain. At the conclusion the prizes were sold by auction, realizing from sixty rupees for a calf to three hundred and fifty rupees for the largest. The tusker and one or two others were ultimately allowed to break through the palisade and return to the jungle.

But previous to these concluding scenes we had retraced our steps to Colombo and Point de Galle, thence to sail eastward, ever eastward, diverging to the north and to the south, yet still eastward, until, guided by Him who rules the seas, we came to the golden West,—the shores of the country to us so precious. And here we close our chapter from "the open volume of the world, upon which," in the words of Lowell, "with a pen of sunshine or destroying fire, the inspired Present is even now writing the annals of God!"

THE END.

www.ingramcontent.com/pod-product-compliance
Lightning Source LLC
Chambersburg PA
CBHW030407230426
43664CB00007BB/778